and *courageous*, for you are the one
all the instruction  de
o their ancestors
strong and *courageous*, for you are
the instructions Moses gave you. Do not dev
I swore to their ancestors I would give them
t. Then you will be successful in everything y
o obey all the instructions Moses gave you. D
e on it day and night so you will be sure to ob
to the left. Then you will be successful in ev
and succeed in all you do. This is My commar
y. Meditate on it day and night so you will be
d or discouraged. For the Lord your God is wit
u prosper and succeed in all you do. This is M
abandon you. Be *strong* and *courage*
t be afraid or discouraged. For the Lord your
possess all the land I swore to their ancestors
ail you or abandon you. Be *strong* and *co*
geous. I will not fail you or abandon you. B
eople to *strong* I swore to their
one who will lead these people to possess all
courageous. I will not fail you or aband
Be *strong* and very *courageous*. Be
u are the one who will lead these people to p
u. Do not deviate from them, turning either to
ive them. Be *strong* and very *courag*
everything you do. Study this Book of Instruc
s gave you. Do not deviate from them, turnin
ill be sure to obey everything written in it. On

To:

DOR

From: with love
always!

Ter

Date:

August 8, 2013

❧

Walking with God

© 2012 Christian Art Gifts, RSA
        Christian Art Gifts Inc., IL, USA

Compiled from *Grace for Each Moment* by Solly Ozrovech and
Promises from God for Purposeful Living.

Designed by Christian Art Gifts

Printed in China

ISBN 978-1-4321-0226-5

13 14 15 16 17 18 19 20 21 22 – 11 10 9 8 7 6 5 4 3 2

Walking
with GOD

christian
art gifts ®

Contents

Introduction

"Be still, and know that I am God." Ps. 46:10

Some days all we want is just a little
more time … And other days we only
need a tender hand to lift us up
and a voice to whisper encouraging words.

Walking with God offers a collection
of short but powerful devotions from
the One-Minute Devotional *Grace
for Each Moment* and a gathering of
best-loved promises from God's
Word to guide and encourage.

In these pages, feel the touch of God's
tender hand and become quiet before Him
so that He can strengthen you for each new
day. Open your heart to the Master Creator,
and discover the encouragement
that can only be found in Him.

I will not fail you or abandon you. Be

the right o

strong and *courageous*, for you

Then you will be successful in

are the one who will lead these people to

you do. Study this Book o

possess all the land I swore to their ancestors

continually. Meditate on it d

I would give them. Be *strong* and very

so you will be sure to obey

courageous, Be careful to obey all the

written in it. Only then will

instructions Moses gave you

and succeed in all you do

Do not deviate from them, turning either to

command be *strong* and *cour*

the right or to the left

Do not be afraid or c

Then you will be successful in everything

For the Lord your God

you do. Study this Book of Instruction

wherever you go. Josh. 1:5

continually. Meditate on it day and night

fail you or abandon you. Be *st*

so you will be sure to obey everything

courageous, for you are t

written in it. Only then will you prosper

will lead these people to possess

and succeed in all you do. This is My

Celebrating Life

Live Life to the Full

For with You is the fountain of
life; in Your light we see light.
Psalm 36:9

Life is the best thing God has given to you. So be grateful for it. When you accept the goodness of life, you will stop fighting against it.

When you accept that life is good, all impatience and frustration will be removed and life becomes a satisfying and exciting experience.

Allow your life to be controlled by godly principles and it will become an expression of those plans. You will possess a unity with the Creator, and your life will be filled with the fullness of God.

Creator God, I thank You that You have a plan
for my life that is filled with the fullness of You.
Amen.

Where Are You Heading?

Thanks be to God, who always leads
us in triumphal procession in Christ.
2 Corinthians 2:14

It is not always easy to choose which road you should follow. But accepting Christ as Lord of your life puts divine powers into action. Your values in Him will provide you with an inspired yet practical goal.

Choosing your goal and objectives with Christ will put you on the right road and will bring joy, confidence and enthusiasm into your life.

If you walk through life in the light of God, the whole journey becomes a joyous experience.

*Dear Guide, thank You that I can
walk through life with You and that
You guide me along the paths of life.
Amen.*

Something to Live For

"Before long, the world will not
see Me anymore, but you will see Me.
Because I live, you also will live."
John 14:19

Many people harbor anxiety because the
future is unknown to them, and become
pessimistic and discouraged. We must
constantly remind ourselves that life is
extremely precious, so that we don't fall into
the trap of depression

Even if the future seems bleak, you can
be assured that your life and future are in
God's hands. God is in control of everything.
There is joy in Christ because He is the Rock
on which you can build your life. His grace
is sufficient to get you through each day.

Seize this life and live it in the abundance
of Jesus Christ your Lord and Savior.

*Through all the changing circumstances of life,
Lord, in joy as well as sorrow, my heart will sing
Your praises and thank You for the abundant life
that You have made possible for me.
Amen.*

An Open Door

"See, I have placed before you an
open door that no one can shut."
Revelation 3:8

Constant grumbling and drudgery makes life
seem meaningless. It doesn't take someone
who lives like this long to wilt intellectually
and to develop a negative, cynical attitude
towards life.

But Christ wants so much more for us.
Scripture, history and personal experience
offer ample testimony to the fact that an
ordinary, seemingly meaningless life can
be transformed by the power of the living
Christ and through His Holy Spirit.

This new life of abundance that Christ
offers you is yours for the taking. Turn to
Christ and He will open the door to a new,
meaningful life for you.

*Lord Jesus, the open door of Your grace leads me
into the abundance and joy of life in Your presence.
Fill my life with new purpose and meaning today.
Amen.*

Experience Christ's Fullness

God was pleased to have all His
fullness dwell in Him, and through
Him to reconcile to Himself all things.
Colossians 1:19-20

Jesus was not just "a good person", He was more than good. He was the personification of perfection.

This breathtaking truth is so overwhelming that we might even hesitate to approach the Lord. But, if He is your Savior, there is no barrier that can separate you from Him. Because of this, life becomes filled with fullness!

Read Ephesians 3:17-18 again, "So that Christ may dwell in your hearts through faith. And I pray that you, being rooted and established in love, may have power, together with all the saints, to grasp how wide and long and high and deep is the love of Christ."

How privileged we are, as God's children, to partake in His festival of love.

*I praise and glorify You, O Loving Savior, that,
through faith, You abide in my heart.
Make it a worthy abode.
Amen.*

Positive Thinking

Be transformed by the renewing of your mind.
Then you will be able to test and
approve what God's will is –
His good, pleasing and perfect will.
Romans 12:2

The teachings of our Lord embraces positive thinking, but it reaches beyond thoughts to touch the hidden possibilities of the spirit.

When we face the reality of situations in our lives, positive thinking can help up to a point, but a relationship with the living Christ can do so much more.

Positive thinking can only bring about limited solutions. Real change comes when you move past thinking, to an unshakable trust of God's work in your life.

Positive thinking, together with solid faith in the Almighty Christ, is a creative force that enables you to live as God intended you to live – in victory and with joy.

Holy Spirit, fill my heart with courage
and the faith to know the good,
perfect and pleasing will of God.
Amen.

Make Today Wonderful

This is the day the Lord has made;
let us rejoice and be glad in it.
Psalm 118:24

Regardless of how bad things appear, God is greater than any situation.

Every day is a unique gift to you from God. What you make of it is your responsibility. The way in which you welcome each new day will depend on your frame of mind and attitude towards life.

Fortunately, your frame of mind is not something that you have to leave in the hands of fate or coincidence. God has given you the ability to choose your frame of mind, as well as the pace of your life. Meet every day with joy and expectation, and then you can live a happy, victorious life!

Father, I experience the reality of Your presence
every moment of the day. Teach me to number
my days in such a way that I will become wise.
Amen.

Find Joy in the Small Things

*Everything God created is good,
and nothing is to be rejected if
it is received with thanksgiving.*
1 Timothy 4:4

Many of us tend to take things for granted – the colors of flowers, the songs of birds, the beauty of a sunrise – these are all things that many people barely notice.

It is only when you begin to contemplate a life without these blessings that you realize how colorless and uninteresting it would be if they were absent. We should cherish and appreciate every blessing in our lives.

We should learn to appreciate the wonders of God's Creation and everything He has granted us through His grace.

*Heavenly Father, I thank You for the everyday
things in my life and for what they mean to me.
Amen.*

Life Is an Open Door

"See, I have placed before you an
open door that no one can shut."
Revelation 3:8

For some people, life is one uninteresting day after another in a meaningless existence.

But it doesn't have to be this way! Jesus has given you the promise of an abundant life. An ordinary, dull life can be transformed by the power of the living Christ through His Holy Spirit. Through the wonder of God's grace, sadness turns into joy, defeat into victory, fear disappears, hate changes to love, and despair to hope.

The moment you accept Christ into your life as Redeemer and Savior, you enter the door of redemption into a new world of vibrant, abundant life.

*Lord Jesus, the open door of Your grace leads
me into a life full of hope and happiness.
Thank You for putting purpose in my days.
Amen.*

Count Your Blessings

*Whoever invokes a blessing in the
land will do so by the God of truth.*
Isaiah 65:16

To the optimist, the simple things in life are a constant source of joy – spontaneous laughter, the bright rays of the sun, and the sounds of the birds in the trees.

People who count their blessings are extremely happy. Even in their darkest moments they maintain a spirit of hope and optimism, because they know things will work out well.

The more you count your blessings, the more it will seem as if God pours them out upon your life. Your heart will overflow with gratitude for God's amazing love. When life becomes a burden and it seems ominously dark around you, recalling your blessings is a sure way to keep a healthy perspective.

*Father, how will I ever be able to express my
gratitude in words? You bless me with so many
things that were I to start listing them one by one,
I would need eternity to thank You.
Amen.*

Seize the Day!

"In the time of My favor I heard you,
and in the day of salvation I helped you."
2 Corinthians 6:2

When you look back on your life, there are certain highlights that tend to stand out – great moments in your life.

The truth is that every day could be a great day in your life if only you appreciated the present and passing moment. Every day is a new birth, with new prospects and opportunities that fall to you from the loving hand of God, so that you can live.

Cherish your memories, but appreciate the importance and wonderful possibilities of today. Accept every moment of every day as a gift of grace from the hand of God and utilize it fully. Then every day will be a great day.

When I am confused and surrounded by darkness,
I know that You will deliver me. You are great
and good and do not scorn my feeble prayers.
Thank You for Your constant presence.
Amen.

Say "Yes" to Life

*"I have come that they may have life,
and have it to the full."*
John 10:10

Every day of your life is a time of boundless opportunity to do good and to grow spiritually and intellectually. Remember, the future belongs to you and you can do with it whatever you want to because God has given you freedom of choice.

God, in His grace, gave you life with a sublime purpose. Every day is a gift from the loving hand of God, but you can only live life to the full when you subject yourself to His purpose for your life.

The abundant life belongs to God and, even though He is generous with this gift, He can only give it to those who are willing to receive and use it. So, say "yes" to life: it is your privilege as well as your responsibility.

*Thank You that I may have everlasting
life through Christ's crucifixion.
Not even death can make me tremble.
Amen.*

Comfort
from God's
Loving Heart

Comfort from God's Loving Heart

He will wipe away every tear from their eyes, and death shall be no more.
Revelation 21:4 ESV

Some people do not believe that Jesus understands human problems. They see the Lord as Someone far removed from our everyday lives and who is only interested in matters of universal importance. Such an attitude reveals a complete misunderstanding of God and His loving concern for the world He created and the people for whom His Son died.

Although God is King of kings and Lord of lords, we must never forget that Jesus is not only our Master, but also our Friend. Because He lived, suffered and died as a human being, He understands human problems and emotions. He also endured suffering, disappointment, sorrow and joy.

The Savior is waiting for you to invite Him to share your life with Him. Open your heart to Him and He will help you in whatever circumstances you may find yourself in.

Through Christ We Are Comforted

Therefore we do not lose heart. Even though
our outward man is perishing, yet the
inward man is being renewed day by day.
For our light affliction, which is but for a
moment, is working for us a far more
exceeding and eternal weight of glory, while
we do not look at the things which are seen,
but at the things which are not seen. For the
things which are seen are temporary, but
the things which are not seen are eternal.
2 Corinthians 4:16-18 NKJV

Yea, though I walk through the valley
of the shadow of death, I will fear no evil:
for Thou art with me; Thy rod
and Thy staff they comfort me.
Psalm 23:4 KJV

"Blessed are those who mourn:
for they shall be comforted."
Matthew 5:4 KJV

"I will not leave you comfortless:
I will come to you."
John 14:18 KJV

This I call to mind,
and therefore I have hope:
The steadfast love of the Lord never ceases;
His mercies never come to an end.
Lamentations 3:21-22 ESV

Who shall separate us from the love
of Christ? Shall tribulation, or distress,
or persecution, or famine, or nakedness,
or danger, or sword? As it is written, "For
Your sake we are being killed all the day long;
we are regarded as sheep to be slaughtered."
No, in all these things we are more than
conquerors through Him who loved us.
For I am sure that neither death nor life,
nor angels nor rulers, nor things present nor
things to come, nor powers, nor height nor
depth, nor anything else in all creation,
will be able to separate us from the
love of God in Christ Jesus our Lord.
Romans 8:35-39 ESV

The Lord is close to the brokenhearted
and saves those who are crushed in spirit.
Psalm 34:18

The eternal God is your refuge,
and underneath are the everlasting arms.
Deuteronomy 33:27 NKJV

"I will not forget you!
See, I have engraved you on
the palms of My hands;
your walls are ever before me."
Isaiah 49:15-16

"I will pray the Father, and He
shall give you another Comforter,
that He may abide with you for ever."
John 14:16 KJV

"Comfort, comfort My people," says your
God. "Speak tenderly to Jerusalem, and proclaim to her that her hard service has been
completed, that her sin has been paid for."
Isaiah 40:1-2

Surely He has borne our griefs and
carried our sorrows; yet we esteemed
Him stricken, smitten by God, and afflicted.
Isaiah 53:4 NKJV

Praise be to the God and Father of our Lord
Jesus Christ, the Father of compassion and
the God of all comfort, who comforts us in
all our troubles, so that we can comfort
those in any trouble with the comfort
we ourselves have received from God.
2 Corinthians 1:3-4

Compassion *from* Our Heavenly Father

Comfort for the Future

*Now the dwelling of God is with men,
and He will live with them. They will
be His people, and God Himself will
be with them and be their God.*
Revelation 21:3

Fear casts a very dark shadow over the future. But when you find refuge in the living Christ, you realize that regardless of how ominous things might appear, everything is still under God's control. The Lord God Almighty still reigns and has not abandoned His Creation.

To believe that God is working out His divine plan, in spite of man's sinfulness, enables you to maintain a well-balanced and calm attitude.

So, you can either look to the future without God and feel depressed and fearful, or you can believe in God's plan of redemption for mankind and approach the future with trust and confidence.

*Eternal God, I believe that You are in control
of this world. Therefore I can face the future
with confidence and hope in Your salvation.
Amen.*

Be a Comforter

They approach and come forward; each helps
the other and says to his brother, "Be strong!"
Isaiah 41:5-6

Life is not easy. But if you complain about
your fate and feel that God has let you down,
you only succeed in creating more misery
and despair.

If the eternal Spirit of the living Christ
lives in you, He will prevent you from
sinking into the quicksand of despair. Cast
your cares upon God. After all, He knows
about everything. Then you will be able to
live creatively and courageously. Through
the power of Christ's indwelling Spirit, you
can triumph over any negative circumstance.

*Powerful Savior, let my faith be so positive
and strong that I will be able to assist
others to overcome their despair.
Amen.*

God Is a Father Who Cares

There you saw how the Lord your God carried
you, as a father carries his son, all the way
you went until you reached this place.
Deuteronomy 1:31

Life is seldom a smooth, problem-free road; times of peace and calm alternate with frustration, disappointments and setbacks.

If you yield to the temptation of being controlled by these feelings, your life will become empty and aimless – robbed of its joy, purpose and meaning.

Nobody escapes the disappointments of life, but people who have faith in the promises of God know that He is with them during the hard times.

When a crisis occurs in your life, the wise thing to do is to turn to God. "Cast all your anxiety on Him, because He cares for you" (1 Pet. 5:7).

*God, in times of crisis, I turn to You
because I know You love me and will
help me, no matter what I face.
Amen.*

Comfort and Strength

May our Lord Jesus Christ Himself
and God our Father, who loved us and by
His grace gave us eternal encouragement
and good hope, encourage your hearts and
strengthen you in every good deed and word.
2 Thessalonians 2:16-17

When Paul wrote this letter to the church in Thessalonica, he was deeply concerned about the persecution they were bound to face.

Paul never sugar-coated true Christian discipleship. Above all, he wanted Christians to be willing to endure affliction for Christ's sake.

This prayer reveals a fatherly concern, prayed from his heart for the congregation because he could not always be with them. He prayed for God to comfort them and to give them strength. These special promises are meant for all God's children. We, too, can draw near to God and ask Him to comfort us and give us strength.

Lord Jesus, comfort our hearts
and give us strength to do
and say only what is right and true.
Amen.

Share Your Burdens with Christ

Cast all your anxiety on Him
because He cares for you.
1 Peter 5:7

There are many aspects of life that can keep us up at night, but it is when we are facing these problems that we must trust God. Jesus promised never to abandon us. He even invites those who are weary and overburdened to come to Him for rest. He will never turn away anyone who comes to Him.

God does not necessarily offer you instant solutions, or make all your problems simply disappear because you pray. But if you place your faith and trust in God and confide in Him in prayer, He will enable you to think clearly and act positively. In His strength you will be able to handle your problems according to the will of God.

Soothe my restless heart, O Holy Spirit.
Calm the tempestuous storms that rage.
Lead me to quiet waters so that
I can experience peace of mind.
Amen.

The Compassionate Jesus

*When He saw the crowds, He had compassion
on them, because they were harassed and
helpless, like sheep without a shepherd.*
Matthew 9:36

Compassion is a distinctive characteristic of Jesus' personality. It flowed from the very center of His heart and filled His teachings. People enjoyed listening to Him and walked many miles just to hear Him. The brief record that we have of what He did and taught in three years reveals the depth of His wisdom and the uniqueness of His revelation of God the Father.

If life has disappointed you, or if you have failed and are filled with despair and have no idea where to turn to for inspiration and strength, remember the compassion of Jesus. In the power of His love He encourages you to persevere and to rebuild your life.

*Compassionate Lord, thank You
for Your love that renews my life.
Amen.*

"Be Still, and Know"

The Lord said to Job: "Will the one who
contends with the Almighty correct Him?"
Then Job answered the Lord:
"I am unworthy – how can I reply to You?"
Job 40:1-4

Job lost everything. He was left with a few friends who tried to understand what had happened to him, but they did not recognize God's eternal wisdom.

God does not need to give an explanation to any of us. His knowledge and might far surpass ours. We might never fully understand His ways, but we should know enough of His loving nature to be able to trust Him.

Bring your difficult questions to God, but be careful that they don't become an excuse to blame Him for your problems. God is righteous and His actions and thoughts are far above your understanding.

*Righteous God, I do not always understand
the things that happen, but I am content in the
knowledge that You have all the answers.
Amen.*

God As Your Guide

Is any one of you in trouble? He should pray.
Is anyone happy? Let him sing songs of praise.
James 5:13

When you confront a problem in life, you must never forget to go to the One who mercifully offered to be your Father, with your distress, anxiety and confusion.

Find consolation and strength in Jesus Christ because He cares for you and He fully understands your distress and anxiety. Go to the throne of mercy and lay your problems before Him. Give yourself fully to Him in serious prayer and supplication. Then experience the serenity and peace of mind that only He can give you.

Thank God that He lays His hands on you, guiding you safely through the labyrinth of life.

God, You are the only true Comforter.
Thank You for inspiring me
and strengthening me time after time.
You are my refuge and my shelter.
Amen.

You Are Special to God

For God does not show favoritism.
Romans 2:11

God has no "favorites". Whether you are an ordinary person, or a celebrity, in God's eyes you are special because you are one of His creatures; His child and He loves you. You are a unique creation of His hand and you have special value in His eyes.

So many people torture themselves with the thought that they are unworthy in comparison to other believers, or that they have disappointed God. But Jesus reached out to both the worthy and the unworthy. They all received His love, care, grace and compassion.

Do not give in to feelings of inferiority or unworthiness. The Redeemer came for the salvation of all people; both the righteous and sinners.

I know that You live and that
You have forgiven my sins.
Through Your precious blood
I have inherited peace.
Amen.

God Is
Always with You

For men are not cast off by the Lord forever.
Though He brings grief,
He will show compassion.
Lamentations 3:31-3

There are some people who believe that they are totally alone in this world. They feel that they have no one to turn to for help and comfort in times of trouble.

Although it is true that some people do not enjoy the warmth of a family life, or the company of intimate friends, it does not mean that they are alone. God is always with us. He even says, "Surely I am with you always, to the very end of the age" (Matt. 28:20).

So if you feel all alone, turn to Jesus this very moment and remember that He will never leave you nor forsake you.

You are so patient, Lord. You will never forsake man in his feebleness, but You will always be by our side in compassion. Thank You for Your presence.
Amen.

Find Strength and Comfort in the Word

*Open my eyes that I may see
wonderful things in Your law.*
Psalm 119:18

Disillusion and dejection are very common today, giving people a melancholy and gloomy outlook on life.

In order for you to live and not merely exist, it is essential to have a positive attitude towards life. When everything goes well, enjoy life and praise God. But when things do not go that well, you need a strong faith to overcome the stumbling blocks and step out triumphantly.

To prevent falling prey to discouragement and pessimism in such times, search the Scriptures for testimony of the work of the Almighty God. You will find many examples of ordinary people who overcame hostile forces in the name of the Lord.

*You reveal Yourself in Your Word.
It is trustworthy, steadfast and unfailing.
Thank You that I may know this Word contains life.
Amen.*

Be a Comforter

They approach and come forward; each helps the other and says to his brother, "Be strong!"
Isaiah 41:5-6

Life is not easy, and there are many factors that contribute to a difficult life.

As a Christian, you are not necessarily free from temptations and problems. However, the difference lies in your approach to these things. Don't just join the choir of moans – that will only create more misery and despair.

If you have the Holy Spirit of the living Christ in you, He will prevent you from sinking into the quicksand of a depressed and negative attitude. You will look for solutions to life's problems, and if the answers escape you, you will be content, in childlike faith, to cast your cares upon Christ. After all, God knows everything about everything and He has a glorious future planned for you.

Lord, help me to remember that You
have a wonderful plan for my life.
Let me take comfort in that.
Amen.

Be Strong!

Say to those with fearful hearts,
"Be strong, do not fear; your God will come."
Isaiah 35:4

We all experience discouragement at some point in our lives. If you feel that your dreams have been shattered and your efforts have come to nothing, do not allow self-pity to sow the seed of discouragement in your spirit.

There are spiritual reserves from which you can draw that will give you hope and a sense of purpose. Do not rely on your own sources of inspiration, because when these fail you will lose your vision and become discouraged.

God is your constant source of inspiration. Remember, you do not fight alone against negative feelings and emotions. God is on your side and He is waiting to pick you up so that you may proceed with joy and be ultimately triumphant.

I thank You heavenly Father,
that through the power of
Your residing Spirit,
I can triumph over discouragement.
Amen.

Run to Jesus

When He saw the crowds, He had compassion
on them, because they were harassed and
helpless, like sheep without a shepherd.
Matthew 9:36

Jesus' compassion was a sign of His greatness, not an indication of weakness. It resided in the center of His heart and His teachings.

Scripture informs us that ordinary people liked to listen to Jesus and that they took long journeys to hear Him. What Jesus told the people revealed how close He was to the Father and how compassionate He was.

If you are feeling overwhelmed by life and full of despair, remember Jesus and His loving compassion. Run to His open arms and allow Him to soothe and comfort you.

*Compassionate Master, let Your love renew
my life so that I may rejoice in Your love.
Amen.*

Encouragement
for the
Daily Journey

Encouragement for the Daily Journey

Let the morning bring me word of Your
unfailing love, for I have put my trust in You.
Psalm 143:8

Most of us have experienced adverse
circumstances that dramatically affec-
ted us, as well as those we love. How often
has your world been disrupted by serious
illness, death, failure or financial disaster?

Nevertheless, you have the assurance of
God's love for you. However despondent
you may be about unexpected events and
circumstances that cause you great anxiety,
never lose sight of the fact that Jesus loves
you with an unfailing, eternal and perfect
love. He will ease your burden if you turn to
Him in prayer and faith. He will allay your
fears and concerns and give you His Holy
Spirit to comfort and lead you.

Regardless of circumstances, or how dark
the future may seem, if you take God at His
Word and listen to His promises, you will
enjoy His blessings as well as His peace that
drives out all fear (1 John 4:18).

Encouragement to Endure

The Lord is my light and my salvation;
whom shall I fear? The Lord is the strength
of my life; of whom shall I be afraid?
Psalm 27:1 KJV

God is our refuge and strength, an
ever-present help in trouble. Therefore we
will not fear, though the earth give way and
the mountains fall into the heart of the sea.
Psalm 46:1-2

Yet the Lord will command His lovingkind-
ness in the daytime, and in the night
His song shall be with me, and my
prayer unto the God of my life.
Psalm 42:8 KJV

Yet the Lord longs to be gracious to you;
He rises to show you compassion.
For the Lord is a God of justice.
Blessed are all who wait for Him!
Isaiah 30:18

For you have need of endurance,
so that after you have done the will of God,
you may receive the promise.
Hebrews 10:36 NKJV

In all my prayers for all of you, I always
pray with joy because of your partnership
in the gospel from the first day until now,
being confident of this, that He who began
a good work in you will carry it on to
completion until the day of Christ Jesus.
Philippians 1:4-6

Count it all joy, my brothers, when you
meet trials of various kinds, for you
know that the testing of your faith
produces steadfastness. And let steadfastness
have its full effect, that you may be perfect
and complete, lacking in nothing.
James 1:2-4 ESV

In this you rejoice, though now for a little
while, if necessary, you have been grieved by
various trials, so that the tested genuineness
of your faith – more precious than gold that
perishes though it is tested by fire – may be
found to result in praise and glory and
honor at the revelation of Jesus Christ.
1 Peter 1:6-7 ESV

Let the morning bring me word
of Your unfailing love, for I have put
my trust in You. Show me the way
I should go, for to You I lift up my soul.
Psalm 143:8

And not only that, but we also glory in tribulations, knowing that tribulation produces perseverance; and perseverance, character; and character, hope. Now hope does not disappoint, because the love of God has been poured out in our hearts by the Holy Spirit who was given to us.

Romans 5:3-5 NKJV

But rejoice, inasmuch as ye are partakers of Christ's sufferings; that, when His glory shall be revealed, ye may be glad also with exceeding joy.

1 Peter 4:13 KJV

There hath no temptation taken you but such as is common to man: but God is faithful, who will not suffer you to be tempted above that ye are able; but will with the temptation also make a way to escape, that ye may be able to bear it.

1 Corinthians 10:13 KJV

Why are you cast down, O my soul? And why are you disquieted within me? Hope in God; For I shall yet praise Him, the help of my countenance and my God.

Psalm 42:11 NKJV

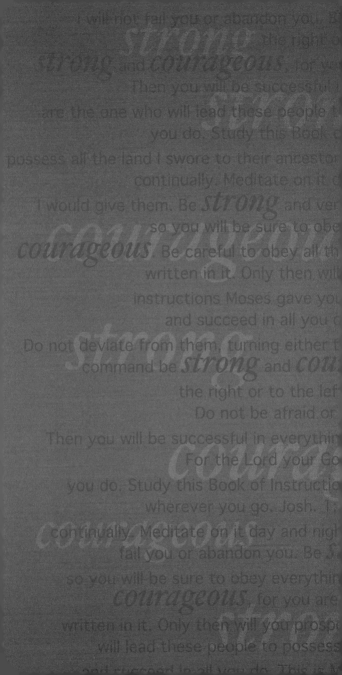

Faith *to* Stand Strong

The Lord Is Our Shepherd

The Lord is my shepherd,
I shall not be in want.
Psalm 23:1

Those of us who belong to the Lord know we are safe and secure. We know for certain that the Lord is our Shepherd and therefore we do not fear the future because our Shepherd is already there. He will walk before us every day, leading us to our eternal destination.

Sometimes we have doubts about the future. We wonder whether we will have enough to provide for our essential needs. With childlike certainty, the psalmist then tells us, "I shall not be in want." You shall not be "in want" of anything that you truly need and that is good for you. The Lord will hear when you call, because His love never changes.

Lord God, it is a glorious reassurance to
me that You are my Shepherd and that
in Your hands I am safe and secure.
Amen.

A Most Enriching Experience

"Remain in Me, and I will remain in you."
John 15:4

It is worth remembering that the stars are still shining, even when clouds hide them. Remember, too, that behind the dark patches of life, the eternal love of your heavenly Father is still shining brightly. If you have cultivated trust in Him, your faith will carry you through the darkest moments of life.

The life that Jesus promises us if we "remain in Him" is such a challenge that people hesitate to accept it and instead choose to remain in a religious rut that promotes neither joy nor spiritual growth.

The life that Christ promises is much more than an emotional experience. It creates inner peace, a constructive purpose in life, and provides the strength to achieve and maintain such a life through the power of the Holy Spirit.

Holy Father, I praise and glorify You for the life-changing strength that flows from Christ. Amen.

Believing without Seeing

Therefore we are always confident.
We live by faith, not by sight.
2 Corinthians 5:6-7

When you are facing problems, difficulties or tough decisions, do you trust God sufficiently to put yourself and your future in His hands?

Jesus came to confirm that God loves you unconditionally. His care, help and compassion are unquestionable. You are precious in His sight. Therefore, Christ will not allow anything to harm you.

With this assurance, you can trust God unconditionally in everything. Then you will walk along His path, doing His will.

If you do this, you will experience peace and tranquility of mind. Even if you cannot see the complete road ahead, faith will carry you through.

Lord, please be with me in the dark days,
and shine the light of Your presence
before me so that I do not stumble.
Amen.

The Light on Your Way

God said, "Let there be light,"
and there was light.
Genesis 1:3

When we look back along the road we have traveled, we tend to focus only on the negative things. Because the past had its share of problems, many people expect the same from the future.

But this is a negative way of looking at life. The prayer of your heart every day should be, "Lead me, O Light of the world!" Jesus Christ is still the Light of the world and He has promised that those who follow Him will never walk in darkness. Take His hand in faith and trust and experience Him as the light of your life.

*God of light and truth, thank You that Your Son
has illuminated my life so that I can walk into
the future in faith and trust. Be my light,
even when darkness falls around me.
Amen.*

Blessed Assurance

Commit to the Lord whatever you do,
and your plans will succeed.
Proverbs 16:3

Planning is important in every area of life. You plan for the future, for your marriage, for your finances and for retirement. Much of our time and energy goes into planning.

There is a way to make planning better, however, but it requires strict spiritual discipline to make it effective and it must be undertaken with sincerity and honesty. It also requires solid faith and trust in God and in His promises.

Whatever your concern may be, lay it before God in prayer with all your fears and expectations, trusting Him completely.

Leave the matter in God's hands. In His own perfect time and way, He will show you how to bring it to pass.

Dear Lord, guide me to follow Your commands
and to fulfill Your will in obedience.
Amen.

God Has a Plan For You

Do not be distressed and do not be angry with
yourselves for selling me here, because it was
to save lives that God sent me ahead of you.
Genesis 45:5

It is often difficult to understand that God
is fulfilling His plan in your life, especially
when times are tough. When Joseph was
sold into slavery, he probably struggled to
discern God's will. Nevertheless, many years
later, he recognized that God had been with
him through it all.

God determines the pattern of your life.
In your present circumstances, difficult as
they might be, hold on to the assurance that
God is busy working out His perfect plan for
your life. Life's darkest moments can become
a testimony of God's perfect purpose for
your life.

*Faithful Guide, I will trust You to lead me
surely along the pathways through life,
even when the dark shadows hide my way.
Amen.*

God's Love Endures

Though I walk in the midst of trouble,
You preserve my life. The Lord will fulfill
His purpose for me; Your love, O Lord,
endures forever – do not abandon
the works of Your hands.
Psalm 138:7-8

You might sometimes feel that God has abandoned you when you needed Him most. But through faith you need to hold fast to what you know is true about God, even when you cannot see any results.

Although we are inclined to plan our whole course through life, we can confess, together with David, "The Lord will fulfill His purpose for me." In the time of his worst trial, David still trusted God to protect him. Be assured that the Lord will never neglect the work of His hands, so even in the dark times, remember that God is faithful and you can never drift too far away from the sphere of His love.

*Loving God, protect me from
the anger of my enemies.
Thank You that there is no end to Your love.
Amen.*

Find Strength in God

O Lord, be gracious to us; we long for You.
Be our strength every morning,
our salvation in time of distress.
Isaiah 33:2

Immediately after praying to God to save Israel, Isaiah describes Israel's distress: the Assyrians rejected their petition for peace, Lebanon was destroyed, and the plains of Sharon resembled a wilderness.

Isaiah's trust in God never faltered. He believed God's promises that He would preserve Israel and deliver His people. Because of this Isaiah could pray with confidence, "Be our strength every morning, our salvation in times of distress."

Like Isaiah, we can depend on God in times of distress and trouble. Call on Him in such times and feel the strength, that can only come from God, descend on you.

Omnipotent and omniscient God,
help me to trust in Your promises.
Be my strength and my salvation each day.
Amen.

Let Jesus Guide You

*Therefore we are always confident
and know that as long as we are at home
in the body we are away from the Lord.
We live by faith, not by sight.*
2 Corinthians 5:6-7

How often have you experienced doubt, loneliness and anxiety? When an important decision has to be made do you find it difficult to make the right choice? If so, you are relying on your own limited insight.

Regardless of the circumstances, put your plans, your doubts, your fears and your problems before the Lord's throne of grace and ask Jesus to be your Guide. Be sensitive to the whisperings and stirrings of the Holy Spirit in your life, and face the future with faith and hope. You can rest assured that the living Christ will be by your side, leading and guiding you.

*Lord, let Your kindly light guide me.
Help me to understand that I should
take life one day at a time and seek
Your guidance in everything I do.
Amen.*

Find Your Strength in God

Be strong in the Lord and
in His mighty power.
Ephesians 6:10

In order to avoid feeling overwhelmed with anxiety and fear, uncertainty and inadequacy, it is essential to cling to Christ and draw your strength from Him. No one else but God knows you and your problems so intimately and completely, God loves you so much that He keeps a vigil of all-embracing love over you.

Armed with the assurance that you are supported and protected by the power, omnipotence, love and mercy of God, you should be equipped to deal with any situation that life might hand you.

*Thank You for providing me with armor and
shielding me against the shrewdness of Satan.
You are my power and my strength.
In You, Lord, I trust.
Amen.*

A Faith That Counts

The only thing that counts is faith
expressing itself through love.
Galatians 5:6

In order to be effective and powerful, faith must be nurtured. You must have an intimate relationship with Jesus Christ and love Him with such sincerity that His presence becomes a living reality in your life.

Set aside precious moments to be with Him. When you possess a living faith that manifests itself in love, you have the basic qualities of a practical, inspired and effective religion that is acceptable to God. Then it is a source of blessing, not only for you, but also for your fellow man.

*Lord, Your Word teaches me to love You with
my whole heart, soul and mind, and to love
my neighbor as myself. Grant me the strength
to abide by these commandments.
Amen.*

Steadfast in Faith

"Now be strong," declares the Lord, "and work.
For I am with you," declares the Lord Almighty.
Haggai 2:4

In the initial exciting phase of a person's born-again life, the Lord's work is done with zeal and enthusiasm. We are filled with the joy of a new life in Christ and we wish to share our feelings and ecstasy with others.

Whatever happens, do not succumb to the temptation to give up your work for Christ. Seek advice, help and guidance at all times but never allow discouragement to paralyze you in your honest pursuit to serve the Lord. Take courage and be steadfast in faith – through the mercy of Jesus Christ you will achieve success.

*Your Creation, Lord, will never perish;
it is everlasting. Grant me the strength
and make me Your servant so that I
may share in the fulfillment of Your will.
Amen.*

I will not fail you or abandon you. B

strong the right o

strong and *courageous*, for yo

Then you will be successful i

are the one who will lead these people t

you do. Study this Book o

possess all the land I swore to their ancestor

continually. Meditate on it d

I would give them. Be *strong* and ver

so you will be sure to obe

courageous. Be careful to obey all th

written in it. Only then will

instructions Moses gave you

and succeed in all you d

Do not deviate from them, turning either t

command be *strong* and *cou*

the right or to the left

Do not be afraid or

Then you will be successful in everythin

For the Lord your Go

you do. Study this Book of Instructio

wherever you go. Josh. 1:

continually. Meditate on it day and nigh

fail you or abandon you. Be *st*

so you will be sure to obey everythin

courageous, for you are

written in it. Only then will you prospe

will lead these people to possess

and succeed in all you do. This is M

Faithfulness

Faithfulness

"Be faithful, even to the point of death,
and I will give you the crown of life."
Revelation 2:10

Christ requires His followers to be faithful. He Himself demonstrated faithfulness when He sacrificed His life on the cross. When Christ asks us to be faithful to death, He also promises us a divine and royal reward: eternal life!

It is easy to be faithful when life is exciting and you are in the spotlight, but you also need to be faithful when the monotonous routine of your everyday duties begins to wear you down. Be faithful when no one sees you – because God sees you.

Be faithful to what is most noble in yourself. Shakespeare said, "To thine own self be true, and it must follow, as the night the day, thou canst not then be false to any man."

Above all, you should be faithful to God. He is the foundation and the Source of all that is good in your life. Without Him, life has no meaning.

Forever Faithful

Know therefore that the Lord your God
is God; He is the faithful God, keeping His
covenant of love to a thousand generations of
those who love Him and keep His commands.
Deuteronomy 7:9

Most men will proclaim every one his own
goodness: but a faithful man who can find?
Proverbs 20:6 KJV

Because of the Lord's great love we are not
consumed, for His compassions never fail.
They are new every morning;
great is Your faithfulness.
Lamentations 3:22-23

His lord said to him, "Well done, good
and faithful servant; you were faithful over
a few things, I will make you ruler over
many things. Enter into the joy of your lord."
Matthew 25:21 NKJV

The Lord is faithful, and He will strengthen
and protect you from the evil one.
2 Thessalonians 3:3

These shall make war with the Lamb, and the
Lamb shall overcome them: for He is Lord
of lords, and King of kings: and they that are
with Him are called, and chosen, and faithful.
Revelation 17:14 KJV

"Whoever can be trusted with very
little can also be trusted with much."
Luke 16:10

No temptation has overtaken you that is
not common to man. God is faithful,
and He will not let you be tempted beyond
your ability, but with the temptation He
will also provide the way of escape,
that you may be able to endure it.
1 Corinthians 10:13 ESV

If we are faithless, He remains faithful –
for He cannot deny Himself.
2 Timothy 2:13 ESV

Let us hold fast the confession
of our hope without wavering,
for He who promised is faithful.
Hebrews 10:23 NKJV

Your mercy, O Lord, is in the heavens;
Your faithfulness reaches to the clouds.
Psalm 36:5 NKJV

God is faithful, by whom ye
were called unto the fellowship
of His Son Jesus Christ our Lord.
1 Corinthians 1:9 KJV

God is not man, that He should lie,
nor a son of man, that He should repent.
Has He said, and will He not do? Or has
He spoken, and will He not make it good?
Numbers 23:19 NKJV

From the east I summon a bird of prey;
from a far-off land, a man to fulfill My
purpose. What I have said, that will I bring
about; what I have planned, that will I do.
Isaiah 46:11

Therefore let those who suffer according
to God's will entrust their souls to a
faithful Creator while doing good.
1 Peter 4:19 ESV

It is good to give thanks to the Lord,
to sing praises to Your name, O Most High;
to declare Your steadfast love in the
morning and Your faithfulness by night.
Psalm 92:1-2 ESV

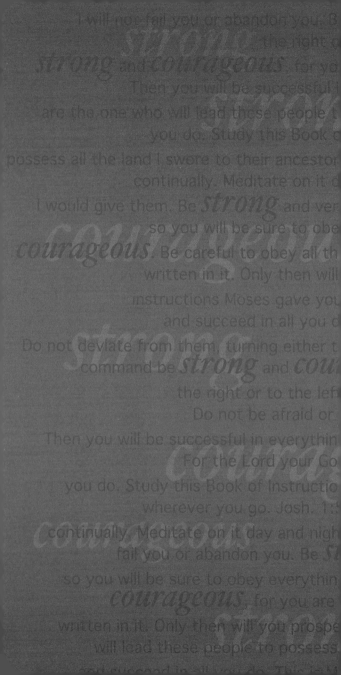

Grace Enough
for You

The Grace of a New Beginning

He who was seated on the throne said,
"I am making everything new!"
Revelation 21:5

It is a sign of God's immeasurable grace that no person ever reaches a stage in life where one cannot start over. Each day that dawns is a new beginning. Our God is the God of second chances.

Do not allow whatever may have happened in the past to cause you to lose sight of what the future may hold. If you wish to make a fresh start, make a firm decision to be done with your old life, even though it will still try to enslave you. All new life comes from God alone. Continually affirm that new life flows through you as a result of God's grace, and you will receive the inheritance of new life that is yours in Christ.

Lord of new beginnings, thank You that each new day Your mercies are new and I can begin again. Amen.

God Works in Everyday Things

In his heart a man plans his course,
but the Lord determines his steps.
Proverbs 16:9

God often works in miraculous ways. We see His glory in the changing heavens; we see His handiwork in the grandeur of Creation.

Yet, God is also the Creator of the small and everyday things: the perfection of the rose and the fragility of the forget-me-not. All these reflect a creative God who is also the Master of order and detail.

We so easily forget that God is interested in our well-being. Just consider how many times He has guided you through difficult circumstances.

Thank You, Almighty God, that You never
cease to work in my life and answer my prayers.
You speak with a thousand tongues;
let me always hear Your voice.
Amen.

Know the Grace of God and Live!

Grace and peace be yours in abundance.
1 Peter 1:2

People are always searching for peace to help them deal with their problems. Do not be tempted to seek man-made solutions, as there is only one true method of handling your life with confidence and assurance – and that is in the power of Jesus Christ.

If you commit yourself and your life to Him unconditionally, then you can rest assured that He will give you the grace required to handle every problem. You will thus be blessed with tranquility and peace far beyond human understanding.

Grace and peace become a reality in your life only through God, so don't drift from Him and forfeit what only He can give.

Loving Master, I thank You, because through Your grace You enable me to face and handle every problem that comes my way.
Amen.

Indescribable Grace

"My grace is sufficient for you, for My
power is made perfect in weakness."
2 Corinthians 12:9

When you find yourself in a situation that
makes you feel incompetent and inadequate,
do not focus on your own abilities. Jesus
made it very clear that we are capable of doing
nothing without Him, but that with Him we
can do anything that needs to be done.

In this truth lies the answer to all your
fears, doubts and insecurities. Whatever
you do in life, first take it to God in prayer,
seek His help and lay all your expectations,
fears and concerns before Him. By allowing
Him to work through you, you will achieve
the kind of success that would otherwise be
unattainable in your own strength.

*Loving Father, I praise You and thank You
for the wonderful assurance that I can do all
things through Christ who gives me strength.
Amen.*

God's Grace Is Sufficient

The days of the blameless are known to the Lord, and their inheritance will endure forever.
Psalm 37:18

We often hear of people who apparently live virtuous lives and yet are plagued by disaster. Sometimes we want to question God's actions, and it is difficult to agree with Paul when he says, "We know that in all things God works for the good of those who love Him, who have been called according to His purpose" (Rom. 8:28).

However, it is important to remember that God's perspective on life is eternal and He truly desires all things to work for your own good. Paul also says that our present suffering does not outweigh the glory that will be revealed in us (see Rom. 8:18). Take courage and let your heart be peaceful – God's grace is sufficient!

I thank You, all-knowing God, that Your grace is always sufficient for me, despite my problems. Amen.

Glory in His Grace

*The grace of the Lord Jesus
be with God's people. Amen.*
Revelation 22:21

The last words of the Bible are this wonderful benediction. How these words soothe our storm-tossed hearts!

We all, at one time or another, suffer from anxiety – either because of a current situation or because we fear the future. In our human weakness and short-sightedness we are not sure how to act. Some people try to handle everything in their own strength, while others throw their hands up in despair.

Remember, the only way out of a problem, and the only reason for success, is the compassionate love and grace of our heavenly Father. The saving and sustaining grace of God permeates our lives. Because He loves you, He blesses you with His grace.

O Lord, I thank You for Your grace.
You saved me and redeemed me from death.
You are my heart's desire.
Amen.

Enough Grace for You

*You then, my son, be strong in the
grace that is in Christ Jesus.*
2 Timothy 2:1

Many people try to flee from the reality of
their personal crises. Regardless of what
your circumstances in life may be, or of how
anxious you are about daunting problems,
don't run away from them in panic and
despair – confront them with Christ at your
side. Receive your strength and confidence
from Him.

No matter how alarming the problem
may seem, you can know for certain that
God's strength will be revealed in your
weakness.

Under all circumstances His grace will
be sufficient for you and you will be able to
deal with your problems with confidence.

*Father, I ask You for strength to carry
the load that is upon me today. Strengthen me
so that I can move forward with confidence.
Amen.*

God's Unfailing Love

"Though the mountains be shaken
and the hills be removed, yet My unfailing
love for you will not be shaken nor My
covenant of peace be removed."
Isaiah 54:10

Most of us have experienced firsthand how the radically changing circumstances of life often have a dramatic influence on us, and on those whom we love. One moment we experience joy, the next we are swept into the depths of despair.

Regardless of these unexpected and unplanned events in your life, you have the assurance of God's love for you. However despondent you may be, never lose sight of the fact that Jesus loves you with an unfailing, eternal and perfect love.

Turn to Him in times of affliction and you will enjoy the blessings of the Lord, as well as His love that drives out all fear.

*Lord, I feel safe in the palm of Your hand.
Thank You for sheltering me when
the storms of life rage around me.
Amen.*

God's Grace-Filled Love

May the Lord direct your hearts into
God's love and Christ's perseverance.
2 Thessalonians 3:5

We cherish in our hearts the eternal truth that God's love is free and undeserved. Nothing that you have done or intend to do can earn you that. God loves you because God is love, and this is a great truth for which we are eternally grateful and for which we should glorify and thank Him.

You are the object of God's love. God Himself lit the flame of love for Him in your heart, so you must do all you can to ensure that nothing extinguishes this inner flame inside you.

Truly, You are love! Your Son became
man to demonstrate true love, Father.
Help me to radiate love in return.
Amen.

Remember God's Share in Your Success

By the grace of God I am what I am,
and His grace to me was not without effect.
1 Corinthians 15:10

There are many people who declare that they are "self-made people" and that their success is solely through their own doing.

It is a foolish person indeed who convinces himself that the honor for his accomplishments is his alone. Everyone faces problems and stumbling blocks in their careers. If God's hand of grace was not shielding you, you would never have triumphed over your problems and adversities.

By gratefully acknowledging God in your achievements, and by thanking Him for His grace and goodness, an extra dimension of joy and happiness that you have not yet experienced will be added to your life.

Thank You for blessing us so
undeservedly and so abundantly, Lord.
You are our salvation and courage for each day.
Amen.

Generosity Is a Gift

Generosity

*Everything comes from You, and we have
given You only what comes from Your hand.*
1 Chronicles 29:14

God gave us the great gift of His Son
and when gifts are given with joy, their
value is enhanced. Every Christian is called
to be a giver. The Holy Spirit teaches you
not to withhold anything that will bless
your neighbor. Your purpose in life is to be a
blessing to others.

When you give someone a gift, pray
that God will bless the receiver. Money or
possessions are not the most important gifts
that you can give. You should develop your
character and personality to God's glory
and use it in the service of others. The world
desperately needs love and kindess. When
you give of yourself, you give the most
generous gift of all.

Do not calculate whether you will profit
from a gift you have given. God gives freely
and you and I should do the same.

Giving and Generosity

I was young and now I am old, yet
I have never seen the righteous forsaken
or their children begging bread.
They are always generous and lend freely;
their children will be blessed.
Psalm 37:25-26

Blessed is he that considereth the poor:
the Lord will deliver him in time of trouble.
Psalm 41:1 KJV

One man gives freely, yet gains even more;
another withholds unduly, but comes to poverty. A generous man will prosper; he who
refreshes others will himself be refreshed.
Proverbs 11:24-25

Each man should give what he has
decided in his heart to give, not reluctantly
or under compulsion, for God loves a
cheerful giver. And God is able to make
all grace abound to you, so that in all
things at all times, having all that you need,
you will abound in every good work.
2 Corinthians 9:7-8

"Give, and it will be given to you. Good
measure, pressed down, shaken together,
running over, will be put into your lap.
For with the measure you use it
will be measured to you."
Luke 6:38 esv

"You must support the weak. And remember
the words of the Lord Jesus, that He said,
'It is more blessed to give than to receive.'"
Acts 20:35 nkjv

Therefore, as ye abound in every thing,
in faith, and utterance, and knowledge,
and in all diligence, and in your love to us,
see that ye abound in this grace also.
2 Corinthians 8:7 kjv

For you know the grace of our Lord Jesus
Christ, that though He was rich, yet for
your sakes He became poor, so that you
through His poverty might become rich.
2 Corinthians 8:9

He who supplies seed to the sower
and bread for food will supply and
multiply your seed for sowing and
increase the harvest of your righteousness.
2 Corinthians 9:10 esv

You will be made rich in every way so
that you can be generous on every occasion,
and through us your generosity will
result in thanksgiving to God.
2 Corinthians 9:11

"And you shall remember the Lord
your God, for it is He who gives you
power to get wealth, that He may
establish His covenant which He
swore to your fathers, as it is this day."
Deuteronomy 8:18 NKJV

Honor the Lord with your wealth and
with the firstfruits of all your produce;
then your barns will be filled with plenty,
and your vats will be bursting with wine.
Proverbs 3:9-10 ESV

God is not unjust; He will not forget
your work and the love you have
shown Him as you have helped His
people and continue to help them.
Hebrews 6:10

He who has pity on the poor lends to the
Lord, and He will pay back what he has given.
Proverbs 19:17 NKJV

Growing *in* Christ

Only Jesus

When they looked up,
they saw no one except Jesus.
Matthew 17:8

Perhaps it is time to pause for a while and examine your spiritual journey under the guidance and leadership of the Holy Spirit. Put all preconceived ideas aside and open up your spirit to His guidance.

It is the all-important sovereignty of Jesus Christ that generates a living faith in your heart. Faith is powerless and meaningless unless it is grounded in Christ and if He rules as King in your life.

If you allow the Holy Spirit to work freely in your life, He will lead you into a deeper and more intimate relationship with Christ. Jesus will begin to occupy the central position in your life.

Desire of my heart, I thank You that my heart thirsts for You all the time. Protect me from anyone or anything that could draw me away from experiencing Your presence in my life. Amen.

Live for Christ

His divine power has given us
everything we need for life and godliness
through our knowledge of Him who called
us by His own glory and goodness.
2 Peter 1:3

The call to live a Christian life rings out once again, but some of us are so overwhelmed by the intensity of the task that our faith falters because of our human weakness.

Yet we do not have to rely on our own abilities to serve God at all. Remember that Christ will not call you to any form of service without equipping you for it. He has set the example and all that He expects from you is to follow Him.

If you commit yourself to Him and place your trust in Him completely, He will provide you with everything that you need to truly live.

Heavenly Father, I dedicate myself to Your service anew, in the certain knowledge that You will provide everything that I need to live an abundant life.
Amen.

To Live for Christ

For to me, to live is Christ.
Philippians 1:21

Too many people live purposeless lives, passing through life with superficial goals. But this type of life cannot bring real satisfaction. Real joy and fulfillment come from having a goal in life that pleases Christ.

Your goal should be to live your life in God's grace, for His glory. You will not be a spiritual person only when the mood strikes you; your faith will remain constant in spite of your fluctuating emotions. Living for Christ means committing your spirit, soul and body to Him.

If you live for Christ, He will be alive to you and you will know the ecstasy of a life poured out before God as a thank-offering. Accept the gift of Himself in your life and allow Him to live through you. Then for you, to live is Christ and to die is gain.

Holy Jesus, live in me so that I
will do all things for Your glory.
Amen.

A Balanced Inner Life

If any of you lacks wisdom, he should ask God,
who gives generously to all without finding
fault, and it will be given to him.
James 1:5

Many people believe that to live a truly spiritual life, you need to live in seclusion; where the realities of life are either ignored or forgotten.

However, the lessons Jesus taught along the dusty roads of Palestine were very spiritual, yet essentially practical. For Him, everything – every thought and deed – was an expression of His relationship with His heavenly Father. Therefore, true Christians do not divide their lives into compartments, because all of their lives should be an expression of the spiritual.

Christianity touches the realities of every day and enables you to look, to a certain extent, at other people's problems as God does.

O Spirit, take control of my life and let everything
I do and say be an expression of my love for You.
Amen.

Growth through Truth

Instead, speaking the truth in love,
we will in all things grow up into
Him who is the Head, that is, Christ.
Ephesians 4:15

If you ignore or undermine the necessity of growth in your spiritual life, it will not be long before you start to suffer on the stormy seas of disappointment and despair. There must be growth and development or your spiritual life will flounder on the rocks.

God makes resources available to us to assist us in our spiritual growth, such as fellowship with believers, Bible study and good deeds, but we should guard against these aids becoming goals in themselves. These are simply the result of our relationship with God and can never be a substitute for our faith in Him.

There can only be spiritual growth if your main objective is to reflect the image of Christ more and more. This should be the heart's desire of every believing Christian disciple.

My Lord, let Your Holy Spirit take possession
of me so that I will live for Your glory alone.
Amen.

Let Others See Christ in You

He said to them, "Go into all the world and preach the good news to all creation."
Mark 16:15

Christians need to be witnesses for Christ. We must not be ashamed of our faith in Jesus Christ. It is, however, important to know when to speak and when to be quiet.

There is one sure way to testify about your faith without offending other people, and that is to follow the example of Jesus Christ. His whole life was a testimony of commitment to His duty, sympathy, mercy, and love for all people – regardless of their rank or circumstances. This is the very best way to be a witness for Jesus.

Ask the Holy Spirit to guide you so that others will see Christ in everything you do and say. In this way you will fulfill the command of the Lord.

Help me, Lord Jesus, to let the Holy Spirit
live through me in such a way that others
may know of Your love for them.
Amen.

Stand by Your Convictions

Simon Peter answered, "You are the Christ,
the Son of the living God."
Matthew 16:16

Many people long for a stronger faith. At one point or another we all need to answer the question that Jesus asked Simon Peter, "What about you? Who do you say I am?"

To benefit fully from the Christian experience, and to know the fullness and abundance of the true life that Jesus offers us, you must have a personal knowledge of the living Christ. This does not only mean learning everything about Him; it means acknowledging Him personally and surrendering your life to Him.

Acknowledge Christ's sovereignty over all creation and abundant life will be yours. That is why Jesus came to this world.

Make me a prisoner of Your love, O Lord,
because only then will I be truly free.
Amen.

Nourish Your Soul

"I am the bread of life. He who comes to Me
will never go hungry, and he who believes
in Me will never be thirsty."
John 6:35

In order to achieve a healthy existence and meet the demands of everyday life, food is essential.

Just as your physical body needs nourishment, so too does your spiritual life. It is an important and integral part of your existence on earth, as well as in eternity. Make sure that you maintain a sustained conversation with Christ so that you can constantly draw on the strength flowing from His everlasting reserves.

In this way you will ensure that your life will be powerfully enriched, because Jesus is living inside you through His Holy Spirit.

*Lord, You are my daily bread and Your truth sets
me free. Thank You for presenting us with the
Word so that we may get to know You better.
Help me to find You therein.
Amen.*

Reach for the Sky!

*I want to know Christ and the power
of His resurrection and the fellowship of
sharing in His sufferings, becoming like
Him in His death, and so, somehow, to attain
to the resurrection from the dead.*
Philippians 3:10-11

Ambition is a commendable characteristic but there is one ideal in life that must overshadow all others: to live in the image of Christ. This must be the greatest ambition of every follower of Jesus and demands complete surrender and commitment.

The pure joy of a life in Jesus Christ cannot be measured. Such a life is priceless and precious. However, this demands a sacrifice. A sacrifice of your thoughts and ambitions must be laid on the altar of the living Christ so that His life can be reflected in you. The abundance of life in Him will be more than enough compensation for your complete surrender to your Savior and Redeemer.

*Lord, I want to follow You and
devote my entire life to Your service.
Amen.*

Grow in Wisdom by Serving God

The fear of the Lord is the beginning of wisdom; all who follow His precepts have good understanding.
Psalm 111:10

To be educated is definitely an advantage in life. However, you can be highly educated and still suffer from spiritual want.

For the Christian, sanctification must always receive priority over education. A person who is in the process of developing spiritually is closer to the heart of God and, therefore, he is more skilled in understanding God's ways.

A spiritual person has discovered the true Source of wisdom in life. There is purpose in his service to God. He possesses peace and inner strength born from the fellowship of the Holy Spirit, and lives his life in such a way that he gains deep-rooted contentment and inspiration from it.

Lord, help me to spend every day in fellowship with You and to experience the fullness of life. Amen.

Reflect God's Glory

Be imitators of God, therefore,
as dearly loved children.
Ephesians 5:1

Most of us have a role model to which we aspire to be like, whether it is a teacher, a parent, an employer or even a friend, we want to be like them.

Yet, there is a much better role model for us, a perfect role model for you and me – Jesus Christ. Never forget that He lived and worked just like us and was subject to all the temptations, frustrations, joys and sorrows to which you and I are subject to.

Allow the Holy Spirit to take control of your life and manage it in a way that is acceptable to God. Then you will display a measure of likeness to Christ that will glorify God.

Lord, transform me into Your image more and more.
Transfigure me so that I may become more like
You in my behavior, thoughts and words.
Amen.

The Person You Can Become

However, as it is written: "No eye has seen, no ear has heard, no mind has conceived what God has prepared for those who love Him."
1 Corinthians 2:9

There are two sides to your personality: the person you are, and the person you would like to be. If these are in conflict with each other, you will experience bitter frustration and disappointment.

There is no harm in dreaming about the heights that you can achieve, provided that you take steps to make your dream a reality. You have the potential for spiritual growth that is beyond your wildest imaginings.

Spiritual greatness can be yours if you live in harmony with God. Your whole life should respond to His love with joy and gratitude.

I pray for inspiration and strength to become all that You created me to be. Help me to grow in You day by day and to fulfill Your vision for my life. Amen.

Renew Your Character

Therefore, if anyone is in Christ, he is a new creation; the old has gone, the new has come!
2 Corinthians 5:17

Most people observe our characters and form an impression based on what they see. Yet, only a few people take the time to develop an agreeable character.

Many people believe that a person's character cannot be changed. This is not true. If this were so, the redeeming love of Christ would have been in vain. Sinners can change into saints and unpleasant people can become amiable when the love of Christ enters their hearts.

When you open your life to Christ, His influence is reflected in your life and a transformation occurs. You surrender yourself to the Lord and through that, your character changes.

Your love is always with me, Lord. Father,
draw me closer into Your circle of love every day.
I want to remain in You.
Amen.

Hope Always

Hope

Let Your steadfast love, O Lord,
be upon us, even as we hope in You.
Psalm 33:22 ESV

Hope, a striking painting by Frederick Watts, hangs in the Tate Gallery in London. A beautiful, blindfolded woman is sitting on top of a globe. In her hand she holds a lute. All but one of the strings are broken. She touches the one string with her finger and bends forward, listening. She is filled with hope – believing the best in the worst possible circumstances.

As long as hope is alive, life cannot get us down; we will not snap under the weight of our problems and afflictions. God is able to turn the worst situations around.

Where hope exists, no night can be completely dark. Hope fills our hearts with joy even when our hearts are breaking.

It is hope that gives us an invincible spirit. This sinful world only knows about a hopeless end; the Christian knows an endless hope!

Hope that will not Disappoint

Why art thou cast down, O my soul?
and why art thou disquieted in me?
Hope thou in God: for I shall yet praise
Him for the help of His countenance.
Psalm 42:5-6 KJV

In hope he believed against hope,
that he should become the father of
many nations, as he had been told,
"So shall your offspring be."
Romans 4:18 ESV

We rejoice in the hope of the glory of God.
Not only so, but we also rejoice in our
suffering, because we know that suffering
produces perseverance; perseverance,
character; and character, hope. And hope
does not disappoint us, because God has
poured out His love into our hearts by the
Holy Spirit, whom He has given us.
Romans 5:2-5

Surely there is a future,
and your hope will not be cut off.
Proverbs 23:18 ESV

May the God of hope fill you with all joy
and peace in believing, so that by the power
of the Holy Spirit you may abound in hope.
Romans 15:13 ESV

God has chosen to make known among the
Gentiles the glorious riches of this mystery,
which is Christ in you, the hope of glory.
Colossians 1:27

This hope we have as an anchor of the soul,
both sure and steadfast, and which
enters the Presence behind the veil.
Hebrews 6:19 NKJV

Therefore, prepare your minds for action;
be self-controlled; set your hope
fully on the grace to be given
you when Jesus Christ is revealed.
1 Peter 1:13

For we were saved in this hope,
but hope that is seen is not hope;
for why does one still hope for what he sees?
But if we hope for what we do not see,
we eagerly wait for it with perseverance.
Romans 8:24-25 NKJV

Hope deferred maketh the heart sick:
but when the desire cometh, it is a tree of life.
Proverbs 13:12 KJV

The eyes of the Lord are on those
who fear Him, on those whose
hope is in His unfailing love.
Psalm 33:18

O Israel, hope in the Lord;
for with the Lord there is mercy,
and with Him is abundant redemption.
Psalm 130:7-8 NKJV

You will feel secure, because there
is hope; you will look around and
take your rest in security.
Job 11:18 ESV

No one whose hope is in You will ever be
put to shame, but they will be put to shame
who are treacherous without excuse.
Psalm 25:3

Lead me in Thy truth, and teach me:
for Thou art the God of my salvation;
on Thee do I wait all the day.
Psalm 25:5 KJV

Hope *and* Trust in God

Hope for the Future

Has He not made with me an everlasting covenant, arranged and secured in every part?
2 Samuel 23:5

Many people look to the future with deep anxiety because they are carrying the heavy burden of their daily responsibilities alone. Unless you have a strong faith, this could have far-reaching effects on your physical, emotional and mental well-being.

The Son of the Most High God died and rose from the dead to set you free from this burden of worry. God loved you so much that Jesus Christ gave His life to redeem you from the terrible burden of anxious worries. Unlike those who have no hope, you are blessed with the assurance that the Savior died in order that you may live. Regardless of the circumstances you're in, this assurance should be a great comfort and encouragement.

I thank You, Lord, that in spite of my circumstances I can praise You, for You are in control and You are ever-faithful. Amen.

Trust God

I heard, but I did not understand. So I asked,
"My lord, what will the outcome of all this be?"
Daniel 12:8

People often find it difficult to understand
God's purpose for their lives – especially
when things go wrong. Their vision of the
future fades and their faith wavers.

The core of a strong faith depends on
your ability to trust God completely, no
matter what happens. The true test of faith
comes when things turn against you; when
you are tempted to question God; when you
are in total despair.

Jesus had an unconditional trust in God.
Even in His darkest moments, His faith was
strong enough to enable Him to fulfill the will
of the Father. Trust God in all circumstances
and the grace of God will help you deal with
every situation.

Lamb of God, I look up to You
to strengthen my faith through the
work of Your Holy Spirit in my life.
Amen.

On Eagles' Wings

Those who hope in the Lord will renew their
strength. They will soar on wings like eagles.
Isaiah 40:31

Too often we get hung up on things that don't really matter and we allow them to distort our view of life.

A positive Christian, however, has the ability to rise above small irritations by trusting in the Lord in all circumstances and by always remaining conscious of His presence. It is impossible to be trivial and small-minded when the love of Christ fills your heart and mind.

Spreading God's love by the power of the Holy Spirit means being able to rise above trivialities and reach the heights that the God of love desires from all His children. Then we can rise up on the wings of eagles and see things from their true perspective.

Holy Spirit, fill me with Your presence and help me to trust in God so I can rise above my problems. Amen.

Unshakable Trust

Be joyful in hope, patient in affliction.
Romans 12:12

When everything seems to be going wrong you may feel overwhelmed by your problems and want to give up or try to solve them in your own strength. But remember, the Lord has promised to never leave nor forsake you.

However, you must have patience because you cannot hurry or prescribe to God. He does everything in His own perfect time and way. God sees the big picture of your life – He is all-knowing and all-seeing.

Ask the Holy Spirit to teach you to wait patiently on the Lord. Then, with childlike trust, you can leave everything in God's hands. Those who stand steadfast in affliction receive God's most precious gifts from His treasure house of mercy.

Lord and Father, I find peace
of mind in trusting You completely.
Amen.

A Life Based on Trust

I have learnt to be content whatever the circumstances. I know what it is to be in need, and I know what it is to have plenty.
Philippians 4:11-12

As a follower of Christ you have powers at your disposal that enable you to tackle life positively and constructively. Remember that dynamic discipleship is based on faith that finds expression in deeds, not in feelings. Focus on the fact that God loves you, even though you might be experiencing the darkest time of your life.

Acknowledge the fact that He will never leave you, even though you may not be able to feel His presence right now. If your life is based on your faith in Christ, your confidence will increase and you will overcome every feeling of inferiority. There will be no situation that you will not be able to handle through Christ's wisdom and power.

I thank You, Lord Jesus, that I can start every day with confidence because I find my strength in You.
Amen.

Plan with God

*So that your faith might not rest on
men's wisdom, but on God's power.*
1 Corinthians 2:5

Have you ever experienced the disappointment of seeing carefully planned dreams fall apart? Many people who experience such a setback are unwilling to take any other risks.

Don't let that happen to you – don't let your potential lie wasted and unused. When you trust God in everything you do and submit to His will and obey Him, you might feel that things move too slowly for you, but be patient. Steadfastly put your trust in God and you will find peace of mind knowing that God is in control and that the fulfillment of your plans will be to your lasting benefit.

*Lord, I know that when I bring my plans for my life
to You, You will show me what Your plans are,
and You will help me to succeed in all things.
Amen.*

Your Divine Companion

The righteous cry out, and the Lord hears them; He delivers them from all their troubles.
Psalm 34:17

Many people struggle with loneliness for a variety of reasons. When you find yourself feeling depressed and lonely, Satan will try to sow seeds of doubt, discouragement and despair in your heart, making you want to give up hope.

But don't give up! The hand of God rests on you always. Rather lay your fears and worries at the feet of the living Christ. Open up your heart and life to the Holy Spirit and He will fan the flame of hope once more, allowing it to burn brightly and light your path.

Powerful Redeemer, grant me the strength to keep my hand firmly in Yours even under the most difficult circumstances. Lead me from the darkness into Your wonderful light. Amen.

Light up Your Life

When Jesus spoke again to the people,
He said, "I am the light of the world.
Whoever follows Me will never walk
in darkness, but will have the light of life."
John 8:12

Darkness can cause fear, depression, lone-liness and sorrow. The darkness of the soul has a similar effect on people. When light comes, it brings relief and a feeling of safety.

The light of hope and peace flickers and dims when we face afflictions and trials. The only way to overcome the darkness is to turn to Christ. Instead of fearing the darkness, light a small candle of faith to brighten it.

Walk in His light and soon you will find that the darkness has passed. With His light in your heart, each day becomes radiant for you.

*Loving Guide, while You hold my hand I am
safe and secure. Strengthen my faith daily.
Amen.*

God's Sufficient Grace

"My grace is sufficient for you, for My
power is made perfect in weakness."
2 Corinthians 12:9

All of us, at one point or another, when
faced with a certain situation feel hopeless
and defeated.

Yet whatever the predicament you are
in, however dark the outlook, never underestimate the extent of God's love for you and
the expanse of His grace. Look at examples
in the Bible or in history when God
transformed despair into hope and defeat
into victory through His grace.

He is waiting for you to turn to Him and
trust in Him. Your faith will be rewarded
and, in His own wonderful way, He will
deliver you.

*God, through the years You have proved Yourself
to be faithful. Therefore I will hold on to Your hand
in the future because Your grace is sufficient for
me at all times and under all circumstances.
Amen.*

Love Fills the Heart with Hope

Brothers, we do not want you to grieve like the rest of men, who have no hope.
1 Thessalonians 4:13

Hope and despair are found in the hearts of people and not in circumstances. Love is so important because it causes hope to triumph. When things are at their darkest, hope rises through love to light the darkness of night. There is no room for despair; God has enough love to avert it. He has woven hope into the nature of man so that we can trust in the future.

When all is hopeless, it is hope that keeps us going. Hope strengthens the soul so that we can hold on to eternity and on to the love of God. His love is infinite; He gives us hope out of love.

Lord, may I never believe that anyone is hopelessly lost, because, in love, You sent Your Son to save the lost. Amen.

Walk in the Light

This is the message we have heard from
Him and declare to you: God is light;
in Him there is no darkness at all.
1 John 1:5

Many things that happen in the world today
are symptoms of a sick society. The average
person feels unable to confront the evil
around him or her, which can give rise to an
attitude of complete despair.

Nothing in our modern world can be as
appalling as the crucifixion on Golgotha.
And yet the Light broke through that darkest
moment in history, when Jesus overcame the
forces of evil and rose triumphantly from
the dead.

Regardless of how dark your circumstances may be, put your trust in Christ,
follow Him and you will see how His light
expels the darkness from your life.

Lord Jesus, in Your light we can see light.
Help us to see Your light in this dark world
so that the darkness will be dispersed.
Amen.

Open the Eyes of My Heart

I pray also that the eyes of your heart may be enlightened in order that you may know the hope to which He has called you, the riches of His glorious inheritance in the saints.
Ephesians 1:18-19

At the time of writing this, Paul was confined to a prison cell in Rome, under the constant watch of the Roman guard. But who could possibly tell from his prayer that anything was wrong! Paul's faithful description of God's power does not allow even a hint of hopelessness or despair to filter through. Instead he talks of the "glorious inheritance" of a future in heaven.

Paul's eventual hope was not in earthly people, but in heaven, eternity and God. The eyes of his heart could see clearly. Are the eyes of your heart open?

Wonderful Redeemer, help me, through Your Holy Spirit, to grasp the wonderful future that You have made possible for me. Amen.

Trust in God Alone

In Him our hearts rejoice,
for we trust in His holy name.
May Your unfailing love rest upon us,
O Lord, even as we put our hope in You.
Psalm 33:21-22

We all need security. When difficult situations threaten to overwhelm us, most of us lean heavily on family and friends for help and support. But this prayer reminds us that, in the long run, only the Almighty God can protect and save us.

It is fitting to admit our dependence on the Lord when we come to Him in prayer. Remember that He is our Shield and Protector. As we focus on this wonderful truth, our fear will turn into praise.

Become quiet for a few minutes and think about the ways in which you seek security, in both big and small situations. Then confess to God that, in future, you will trust fully in Him alone.

Lord Jesus, our hope and salvation, surround us with Your unfathomable love and protection. Amen.

Joy Found
in the Lord

Jesus, the Source of Happiness

Hosanna! Blessed is He who comes in the name of the Lord! Blessed is the coming kingdom of our father David!
Mark 11:9-10

To be blessed we must know Jesus as our personal Savior and Redeemer; we must commit our lives to Him and be obedient to His will.

We all search for happiness, on our own terms, and because of this we run the risk of missing Christ's blessing. Man's happiness often depends on chance or luck: a sudden change in our condition. It is something that life offers and then, just as suddenly, rips away.

Man calls it happiness when things go his way for a while, but Christ's happiness is a happiness that is different; it is a joy in Him.

Lord Jesus, I praise Your glorious name for You are the source of all my happiness because You delivered me and made me a child of God.
Amen.

God's Joy

"No one will take away your joy."
John 16:22

The world's joy is temporary and transitory; Christ's joy is a deep well of quiet happiness and, because the source of it is the Lord Himself, it is stable and steadfast.

In the eyes of the world there may be no outward reason for joy, but with Christ's peace that fills our lives and our hearts, we can rest assured that His eternal fountain of inner joy will never run dry and that no one can take it away. Everlasting joy is ours. The Savior Himself promises us that.

Holy Spirit of God, thank You that one of Your gifts is joy. Let me never disappoint my Lord by being a despondent Christian.
Amen.

True Holiness

"My thoughts are not your thoughts, neither
are your ways My ways," declares the Lord.
Isaiah 55:8

To many people it seems inconceivable that
a life of fullness and great joy can be likened
to holiness. Yet true holiness is the most
dynamic, creative and meaningful lifestyle
in the world.

To be holy implies that you live in a right
relationship with God. It causes you to enjoy
life to the full and also gives you a greater
understanding of people.

The secret of a balanced, joyful, rewarding
life is to live in such a way that it is easy for
the Lord to reveal Himself through you. This
is the way of true sanctification, but is also
the road to a successful life according to
God's standard.

*Teach me, O Holy Spirit, the true meaning of
holiness and enable me to live a life that will
bring glory and honor to You each day.
Amen.*

Experience the Joy of the Lord!

Then the people of Israel – the priests, the Levites and the rest of the exiles – celebrated the dedication of the house of God with joy.
Ezra 6:16

Serving God and worshiping Him are not simply duties to perform but actually awesome privileges. Regular attendance of services or places of worship must never be allowed to turn you into a passive spectator. During times of worship, remember that you are in the presence of the most holy God.

Enjoy your life with Christ. Allow Him to become part of your daily life. Then you will discover the fullness of life that He offers you.

Lord, I want my worship to be filled with an awareness of Your holiness. Help me to never lose sight of who You truly are.
Amen.

Our Calling to Cheerfulness

Rejoice in the Lord always.
I will say it again: Rejoice!
Philippians 4:4

Christians are supposed to rejoice, and if joy fills our lives, we will reap rich rewards spiritually. Many people spread gloom and doom wherever they go, but as a child of God, you can spread joy and inspiration because Christ has given us an indestructible joy that carries us through life.

When you are spiritually sensitive, you have no reason to be despondent. Your daily walk with Jesus Christ, the glorious promises in His Word and God's profound mercy will fill your life with joy, purpose and direction.

Your cheerfulness is not a façade that you put up to impress people but comes from a heart and mind that are in harmony with God through Jesus Christ.

Lord, You fill my days with joy. Your peace flows through me like a quiet stream. Amen.

Happiness in Christ

He who has clean hands and a pure heart, who
does not lift up his soul to an idol or swear by
what is false. He will receive blessings from the
Lord and vindication from God his Savior.
Psalm 24:4-5

No one can take away the joy and blessings
that Christ gives us. We can find joy in Christ
even when we are in pain. This joy cannot be
erased by sorrow, loss, disappointment, or
failure. It is a happiness that sees a rainbow
through tears.

The joy that is found in Christ does
not depend on our circumstances. It is a
deep, everlasting and steadfast joy. It is not
something that we can strive for and attain
through any human endeavor. It is a gift of
God's grace.

The Holy Spirit will strengthen and guide
us to obey Christ, so that His happiness and
blessing will become our portion.

*Loving Master, thank You that the joy You give
is steadfast and indestructible – unlike the
temporary and transient happiness of the world.
Amen.*

Fulfillment in Christ

As the deer pants for streams of water,
so my soul pants for You, O God.
My soul thirsts for God, for the living God.
Psalm 42:1-2

The same longing that moved the psalmist's heart is evident in the hearts of people today. Although they desire to know God, they wander blindly along paths that do not lead to Him, finding no joy or satisfaction.

However, those who are truly wise know that true satisfaction and fulfillment are to be found only in spiritual things. A proper balance between material and spiritual aspects of life must be maintained; and this is only possible when Christ is at the center of your life.

The Lord cares about every aspect of your life, and when you taste and see that He is good, your life will be rich and fruitful.

*Living Savior, in You alone I find fulfillment
and satisfaction. Praise Your holy name.
Amen.*

Serve the Lord Joyously

The joy of the Lord is your strength.
Nehemiah 8:10

There are times in our lives when we feel powerless and grief seems to take hold of our hearts.

Note that our verse today does not state that our joy lies in our own strength. Rather, it says that we have the Lord's joy. What could be better than that?

Our feelings are uncertain and unstable, but the Lord never changes. He is always there, but we must not allow clouds of uncertainty to hide His face. It is a precious assurance for every believer – I serve the Lord joyously and He shelters me.

Please, Lord Jesus, let me serve You with happiness and joy and, in so doing, become a powerful testimony of You in this dismal world. Amen.

The Joy of Faith

He who unites himself with the
Lord is one with Him in spirit.
1 Corinthians 6:17

Joy and gladness are not the main goals of the Christian faith, but important by-products of it. The focus and purpose of our faith is the Lord Himself. When His life-giving Spirit fills your heart, the joy of a Christ-filled life becomes yours.

Forgiveness and a Spirit-filled life bring great joy to all who strive to live in Christ. And the culmination of this joy is to live in the constant awareness of the presence of God. You find yourself in fellowship with Him at all times, in all places. The more you become aware of His closeness, the stronger and more meaningful your faith gets. Then joy, unspeakable and full of glory, will flow from you.

Father, I want to express my
gratitude to You for Your closeness by
living a life that glorifies You in every way.
Amen.

Be Cheerful

Rejoice in the Lord always.
I will say it again: Rejoice!
Philippians 4:4

Cheerfulness is a Christian obligation and, if we measure up to it, it brings rich dividends in our spiritual lives. As a child of God, you can experience the joy and inspiration of the living Christ in your life, enabling you to overcome all moodiness when others hassle you, and to rejoice in the spiritual experience that transforms depression into true cheerfulness.

Your daily walk with Jesus Christ, the glorious promises contained in His Word, the experience of God's profound mercy that transcends understanding; these will fill your life with joy, purpose and direction.

Lord, Your joy is my strength. Even when I suffer, I know that You will deliver me.
Amen.

Kindness

I will not fail you or abandon you. Be ... left. Do not deviate from them, turning ... **strong** and *courageous*, for you ... ything the right or to the left. ... are the one who will lead these people to ... uction Then you will be successful in ever... ...ossess all the land I swore to their ancestors ... night you do. Study this Book of Instructio... I would give them. Be **strong** and very ... ything continually. Meditate on it day and nig... *courageous*. Be careful to obey all the ... ...osper ...ou will be sure to obey everyth... ...es gave you. ... is My written in it. Only then will you prospe... Do not deviate from them, turning either to ... ...ous and succeed in all you do. This is ... **strong** the right or to the left. ...raged, command be **strong** and *coura*... Then you will be successful in everything ... ...h you. Do not be afraid or discouraged. you do. Study this Book of Instruction ... will not For the Lord your God is with you. continually. Meditate on it day and night **g** and wherever you go, Josh. 1:5-9. I will n... ...so you will be sure to obey everything ...e who fail you or abandon you. Be **strong** written in it. Only then will you prosper ...land I *courageous*, for you are the on... and succeed in all you do. This is ...

Kindness

A kind man benefits himself,
but a cruel man brings trouble on himself.
Proverbs 11:17

Kindness, as it is used in the Bible, means to be kind-hearted. It is the good-naturedness of love. There are many Christians who are good people, but who tend to be unkind and constantly critical of everything.

The kindness of love strives for fairness toward God and your fellow man. In essence, faith requires loyalty and reliability and both are born from the love of God.

Kindness seeks only the best for your fellow man, regardless of what he may do. It discards all bitterness and thoughts of revenge and lives in peace with everyone.

Love that is kind must be the distinctive characteristic of Christ's followers. Only then will we succeed in being His witnesses. Our kindness must be evident to all people; they will then ask about the source of our kindness and so find Jesus.

Kindness Accomplishes Much

He did good by giving you rains from
heaven and fruitful seasons, satisfying
your hearts with food and gladness.
Acts 14:17 ESV

"Then the King will say to those on His right,
'Come, you who are blessed by My Father;
take your inheritance, the kingdom prepared
for you since the creation of the world.
For I was hungry and you gave Me
something to eat, I was thirsty and you
gave Me something to drink, I was a
stranger and you invited Me in, I needed
clothes and you clothed Me, I was sick
and you looked after Me, I was in
prison and you came to visit Me.'"
Matthew 25:34-36

Do you show contempt for the riches
of His kindness, tolerance and patience,
not realizing that God's kindness
leads you toward repentance?
Romans 2:4

Finally, all of you be of one mind, having
compassion for one another; love as
brothers, be tenderhearted, be courteous.
1 Peter 3:8 NKJV

If you spend yourselves in behalf of the
hungry and satisfy the needs of the oppressed,
then your light will rise in the darkness,
and your night will become like the noonday.
Isaiah 58:10

Be ye kind one to another, tenderhearted,
forgiving one another, even as God
for Christ's sake hath forgiven you.
Ephesians 4:32 KJV

Blessed are the merciful,
for they shall obtain mercy.
Matthew 5:7 NKJV

You have granted me life and favor,
and Your care has preserved my spirit.
Job 10:12 NKJV

"Do to others as you would
have them do to you."
Luke 6:31

Blessed is he who is generous to the poor.
Proverbs 14:21 ESV

An anxious heart weighs a man down,
but a kind word cheers him up.
Proverbs 12:25

The Lord's servant must not
be quarrelsome but kind to everyone,
patiently enduring evil.
2 Timothy 2:24 ESV

He who is kind to the poor lends
to the Lord, and He will reward
him for what he has done.
Proverbs 19:17

Giving all diligence, add to your faith virtue;
and to virtue knowledge; and to knowledge
temperance; and to temperance patience;
and to patience godliness; and to godliness
brotherly kindness; and to
brotherly kindness charity.
2 Peter 1:5-7 KJV

Put on then, as God's chosen ones,
holy and beloved, compassion, kindness,
humility, meekness and patience.
Colossians 3:12 ESV

I will not fail you or abandon you. B

strong

the right o

strong and *courageous*, for yo

Then you will be successful i

are the one who will lead these people t

you do. Study this Book o

possess all the land I swore to their ancestor

continually. Meditate on it d

I would give them. Be *strong* and ver

so you will be sure to obe

courageous. Be careful to obey all th

written in it. Only then will

instructions Moses gave you

and succeed in all you d

strong

Do not deviate from them, turning either t

command be *strong* and *cour*

the right or to the left

Do not be afraid or

Then you will be successful in everythin

For the Lord your Go

you do. Study this Book of Instruction

wherever you go. Josh. 1:

continually. Meditate on it day and nigh

fail you or abandon you. Be *st*

so you will be sure to obey everything

courageous, for you are

written in it. Only then will you prospe

will lead these people to possess

and succeed in all you do. This is

Loving Shelter

Divine Protection

They remembered that God was their Rock,
that God most High was their Redeemer.
Psalm 78:35

Many times in the history of the world it seemed as if all was lost and all hope was gone.

Yet God has saved people and nations from devastation in miraculous ways, and has enabled them to overcome dangers and transform defeat into glorious victory.

These cases should serve as a constant reminder of the victorious omnipotence of God in all spheres of life. No circumstances are too small or too big for Him, and no prayer will remain unheard or unanswered. Only in Him will you find deliverance from your distress.

*Lord my God, You are a safe fortress to me,
a shield against every calamity that
threatens to overwhelm me. Knowing this,
I step with confidence into the unknown.
Amen.*

I Am with You!

"When you pass through the waters,
I will be with you; and when you pass through
the rivers, they will not sweep over you.
When you walk through the fire, you will not
be burned; the flames will not set you ablaze."
Isaiah 43:2

It requires great faith and a strong character to be able to work through adversity and disappointment. Many seemingly strong people eventually collapse under their burdens.

The Lord never promised that our lives would be trouble-free just because we choose to serve Him. But He did promise to be there for us at all times, and help us over life's hurdles. Knowing that you don't have to tackle the afflictions of life on your own is a comforting and reassuring thought.

When problems mar your view and place pressure on you, turn to Christ. He is your heavenly Companion. Overcome your problems in the peace of His presence.

Thank You, omnipotent Father, that I can say
with confidence that You are with me day by day.
Amen.

A Safe Haven

*The Lord is my rock and my fortress
and my deliverer; my God, my strength,
in whom I will trust; my shield and
the horn of my salvation.*
Psalm 18:2 NKJV

We all seek shelter at one time or another. It may be in the security of your home, or a shelter against the wind and rain.

Our spiritual and intellectual faculties are also often ravaged by the storms of life. We all need a safe and secure haven where we can find shelter from these storms and be protected from devastating emotional consequences.

Even when it seems as if everything is lost, entrust yourself to the love of Jesus Christ. However dark the road ahead may seem, Christ, in His love, is your shelter and safe haven.

*Thank You, my God, that I find shelter in You
and that I will be safe now and for all eternity.
Amen.*

God Is a Refuge

Is any one of you in trouble? He should pray.
Is anyone happy? Let him sing songs of praise.
James 5:13

When we face a crisis, prayer is sadly only used as a last desperate act when all other efforts have failed.

Even though we are encouraged to call on God throughout Scripture, the average person looks for human solutions first, rather than considering God's loving invitation. Over and over He promises His assistance and grace to those who call on Him in their time of need.

Regardless of what the crisis in your life may be, lay your problem before Him in trust and He will transform your crisis into a blessing.

Father, I am experiencing a crisis. Give me
Your peace so that I can see things from
Your perspective and make the right decisions.
Amen.

A God Who Encourages

May the God who gives endurance and
encouragement give you a spirit of unity
among yourselves as you follow Christ Jesus.
Romans 15:5

If you reach the point in life where you feel discouraged and unable to cope, it is good to spend quality time in the presence of God. There you will receive the encouragement that only He can give.

Be still and surrender yourself anew to Him, and remember that He is God. In the silence of His divine presence, you can recall all His glorious promises of encouragement. Remember that in both the storm and the stillness, God is with you. He does not want you to remain in the dark valley of despondency; He will give you the strength to complete the task He has set before you.

Holy God, when life is too much for me,
I withdraw into Your presence and there I
find the comfort and the strength that I need.
Amen.

God Hears My Cry

I call to the Lord, who is worthy of praise,
and I am saved from my enemies.
2 Samuel 22:4

There is no greater feeling than arriving home safely after a dangerous journey. We like to tell others about our adventures, but we often forget to worship God with prayers of praise for granting us safe passage.

When God delivers us out of desperate situations, we should remember to come quietly before Him for a while and thank Him for what He has done.

How many evils does God protect us from daily? How often have we felt His loving protection over our lives and our loved ones? How can we then forget to thank Him in prayerful worship?

I worship You, Lord my God, because
You have saved me from so much evil.
Amen.

My Help Comes from the Lord

O Lord, how many are my foes! How
many rise up against me! Many are saying of me,
"God will not deliver him." But You are a shield
around me. I lie down and sleep; I wake again,
because the Lord sustains me.
Psalm 3:1-3, 5

If enemies are pursuing you and trying
to make you doubt the power of God's
deliverance by saying, "God will not
deliver you," then do what David did – call
on God, who is your shield and protection.
If you do this, then you will be able to lie
down and sleep in peace, because God will
watch over you.

There is no need to ever be afraid because
God is our protector. He always looks after
His children; He will never stop looking
after us.

*Lord, my loving God, I know that You watch
over me because You are my shield and protection.
Amen.*

God Is My Refuge

Your word is a lamp to my feet
and a light for my path.
Psalm 119:105

In this Scripture verse, the lamp symbolizes the guidance, wisdom and knowledge that we find in the Word. This life is like a dark wilderness through which we must find a way and, just as a lamp helps a traveler in the dark, the Word is a light on our path so we will not stumble.

Pray for light and truth from God's Word so that you can stay on the path of life. Ask God to guide you through the situations that could become stumbling blocks on your spiritual path and commit yourself anew to Him and His Word today.

Thank You, merciful God, that You light up our dark path with the light of Your Word. Help us to use Your light each day. Amen.

Let Your Hand Rest on Your People

Revive us, and we will call on Your name.
Restore us, O Lord God Almighty; make Your
face shine upon us, that we may be saved.
Psalm 80:18-19

When you come to the end of your own reserves and find yourself worn out, there is only one place to which you can flee for refuge. God is your only hope for strength.

God created you to fellowship with Him; He wants you to call on His name. You are the branches of His vine and therefore you are completely dependent on the One who planted you – God Himself.

Thank God for the refuge He offers you and for the love that He showers on you. And when you feel that you cannot go any further, ask Him once again to renew your strength for the road that you must follow.

Provider God, let Your holy countenance shine
down on us in love and provide our basic needs.
Amen.

Rest in God's Care

Show the wonder of Your great love, You who save by Your right hand those who take refuge in You from their foes. Keep me as the apple of Your eye; hide me in the shadow of Your wings.

Psalm 17:7-8

You are the apple of the Lord's eye. God will protect you because He will answer your cries of distress; He is bending down, compassionate and interested in your prayer.

Believe in your heart that God will use His power to protect you. When you look to God with expectation, you receive the protection you so desperately seek.

Let this Scripture verse remind you that God is willing and able to protect you faithfully. He is the only One who can truly shield and protect you, so lay your cares at His feet.

I thank You, Almighty God, that You protect me as the apple of Your eye. Hide me in the shadow of Your wings. Amen.

Take Refuge in God

I will sing of Your strength, in the morning
I will sing of Your love; for You are my fortress,
my refuge in times of trouble. O my Strength,
I sing praise to You; You, O God,
are my fortress, my loving God.
Psalm 59:16-17

Love between people can be a source of great joy or of great pain – especially if someone's love is fickle and unpredictable. However, with God as your Savior, you need never feel that His love is fickle. In contrast to human love, God's love is infallible!

Because of this you can count on God to always be your refuge in times of trouble. When you experience difficult times, find your power, strength and refuge in the infallible love of God. It will never fail you.

Holy God, I seek Your shelter in times of difficulty and affliction. As I turn to You, let me experience Your infallible love.
Amen.

When Dark Clouds Gather

Surely God is my salvation; I will trust and not be afraid. The Lord, the Lord is my strength and my song; He has become my salvation.
Isaiah 12:2

It would be extremely naïve to think that ominous clouds will never gather to darken our lives. It would be even more futile to try and ignore them, hoping they will just disappear, because the storm usually erupts – whether you want it to or not.

With God at the center of your life, however, you will be able to maintain balance at all times. The ominous clouds might still be present, but you will always see the silver lining, and you will have the steadfast knowledge that, behind every cloud, there is a loving Father who is still carving the holy design of your life because He loves you with a divine love.

Even when everything around me is shrouded in darkness, You will shield me. Thank You for supporting and shielding me through Your love – even though I do not deserve it. Amen.

Our Loving Protector

For the eyes of the Lord range throughout
the earth to strengthen those whose
hearts are fully committed to Him.

2 Chronicles 16:9

Let us never think that we have drifted out of the sphere of God's love. We read in His Word that His eyes range throughout the earth in order to help those who put their trust in Him. The Lord always knows who places their expectations in Him: He shelters them in times of danger, helps them handle temptations and problems, and comforts them in their sorrow.

What a blessed privilege it is to have such a God as our protector. Wherever we find ourselves while living within His will, we can rest assured that His eyes keep a loving watch over us and that He is ready to hear when we call and to help when we need Him.

We praise Your great name, God, because
You never forsake those who trust in You.
Amen.

God Performs His Wonders through You

Cast all your anxiety on Him
because He cares for you.
1 Peter 5:7

Sometimes worries beyond your control prey on your mind; you may be concerned about your job, or an increase in rent. If you are anxious and worried about a personal matter, you must remember that God is greater than all the circumstances and situations that could befall you.

For a moment you may have allowed fear and uncertainty about the future to obscure your image of God. However, He is forever constant and He desires to share the deepest experience of your life with you. God's omnipotence will sweep away all petty thoughts and all uncertainty will disappear.

Your works are perfect, Lord, and even
when I drink from the cup of bitterness;
You will never forsake me but will help me
to understand that, with You, I will survive.
Amen.

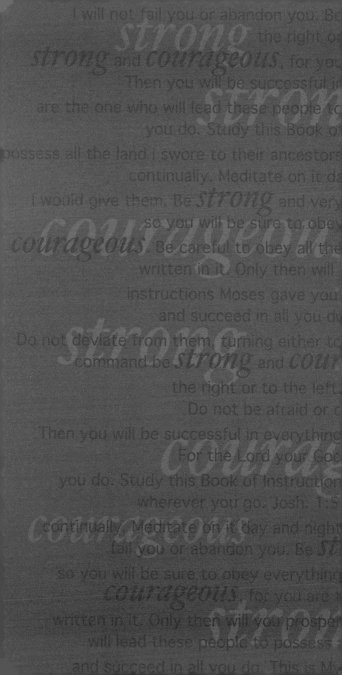

I will not fail you or abandon you. Be
strong
the right o
strong and *courageous*, for you
Then you will be successful i
stron
are the one who will lead these people to
you do. Study this Book o
possess all the land I swore to their ancestors
continually. Meditate on it da
I would give them. Be *strong* and very
so you will be sure to obey
courageous. Be careful to obey all the
written in it. Only then will
instructions Moses gave you
and succeed in all you do
Do not deviate from them, turning either to
command be *strong* and *cour*
the right or to the left.
Do not be afraid or d
Then you will be successful in everything
coura
For the Lord your God
you do. Study this Book of Instruction
wherever you go. Josh. 1:5
coura
continually. Meditate on it day and night
courageous
fail you or abandon you. Be *st*
so you will be sure to obey everything
courageous, for you are t
stron
written in it. Only then will you prosper
will lead these people to possess
and succeed in all you do. This is M

Overcoming *in* Christ

Overcoming in Christ

For everyone born of God overcomes
the world. This is the victory that has
overcome the world, even our faith.
1 John 5:4

Circumstances often fill us with fear and we wonder how we could possibly have landed in such situations.

Traumatic experiences, dramatic changes in our personal lives or even mundane everyday problems might cause us to feel lost and seriously threatened.

The only way we could possibly cope with life is in partnership with God. He created each one of us. He sent His Son to die so that we may have eternal life. Therefore He will not allow you to be defeated. He will deliver you from evil.

It is crucial for you to have an intimate relationship with Him. Then His Holy Spirit will work in and through you and you will be able to live victoriously in His Name.

Victorious Living

"Fear not, for I am with you; be not dismayed,
for I am your God. I will strengthen you,
Yes, I will help you, I will uphold you
with My righteous right hand."
Isaiah 41:10 NKJV

"I have said these things to you,
that in Me you may have peace.
In the world you will have tribulation.
But take heart; I have overcome the world."
John 16:33 ESV

What shall we then say to these things?
If God be for us, who can be against us?
Nay, in all these things we are more than
conquerors through Him that loved us.
Romans 8:31, 37 KJV

Then Jesus said to him, "Be gone, Satan!
For it is written, 'You shall worship
the Lord your God and
Him only shall you serve.'"
Then the devil left Him, and behold,
angels came and were ministering to Him.
Matthew 4:10-11 ESV

The God of peace will soon crush
Satan under your feet. The grace of
our Lord Jesus be with you.
Romans 16:20

Thanks be to God, who gives us the
victory through our Lord Jesus Christ.
1 Corinthians 15:57 ESV

For the weapons of our warfare
are not carnal but mighty in God
for pulling down strongholds.
2 Corinthians 10:4 NKJV

Finally, be strong in the Lord and in
His mighty power. Put on the full armor
of God so that you can take your
stand against the devil's schemes.
Ephesians 6:10-11

Having disarmed the powers and authorities,
He made a public spectacle of them,
triumphing over them by the cross.
Colossians 2:15

You are of God, little children, and have
overcome them, because He who is in you
is greater than he who is in the world.
1 John 4:4 NKJV

A bruised reed He will not break,
and a smoldering wick He will not snuff out,
till He leads justice to victory.
Matthew 12:20

Submit yourselves therefore to God.
Resist the devil, and he will flee from you.
James 4:7 KJV

With God we shall do valiantly;
it is He who will tread down our foes.
Psalm 60:12 ESV

When the perishable has been clothed
with the imperishable, and the mortal with
immortality, then the saying that is written
will come true: "Death has been swallowed
up in victory." "Where, O death, is your
victory? Where, O death, is your sting?"
The sting of death is sin, and the power of
sin is the law. But thanks be to God! He gives
us the victory through our Lord Jesus Christ.
1 Corinthians 15:54-57

He holds victory in store for the upright.
Proverbs 2:7

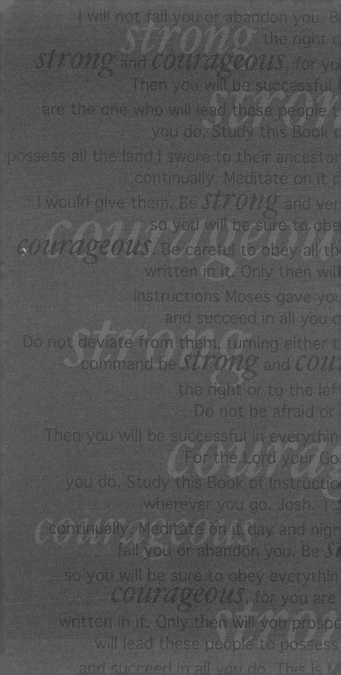

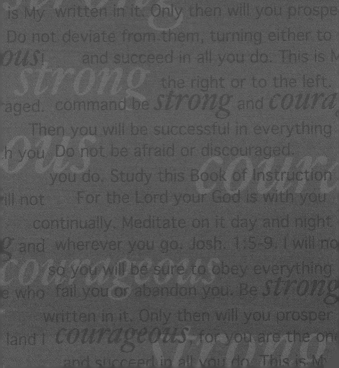

Peace *in* God

It Is Well with My Soul

Why have You rejected us forever, O God?
Why does Your anger smolder
against the sheep of Your pasture?
Psalm 74:1

There are many people whose lives fall apart, and they feel abandoned and forsaken. Yet it is not true to believe that God will ever forsake you. He has promised to be with you always and to never leave you (Heb. 13:5). He even proved His unfathomable love by sacrificing His only Son on the cross for us.

God has a divine purpose for everything that happens in your life. Even when you are the victim of adversity, don't despair. He wants to use these circumstances to bring about His perfect will in your life.

Be still, my soul, the Lord is on your side.
Patiently bear all sorrow and grief and leave all
decisions in His loving hands. When everything
else fails, You, Lord, remain faithful.
Amen.

Light in the Darkness

To those who have been called, who are loved
by God the Father and kept by Jesus Christ:
Mercy, peace and love be yours in abundance.
Jude 1-2

It seems as if the world is in a perpetual state of chaos. Lawlessness and violence are increasing, and people live in fear and insecurity. What is the solution to such a sad state of affairs?

There can only be one answer and that is to turn to Jesus Christ. He has already conquered this dark and hostile world and replaced fear with love so that You can confidently place your faith and trust in Him.

Believe in Jesus and His promises and He will give you the blessing of His peace that transcends all understanding. Trust in Him and He will lead you from the darkness into the light of His immeasurable love for humankind.

Thank You, my Lord and God, that You grant
perfect peace to Your children in this dark world.
Amen.

God Is with You

"The Lord your God is with you, He is mighty
to save. He will take great delight in you."
Zephaniah 3:17

When things go wrong in life it is easy to
despair and become overwhelmed by a sense
of complete helplessness and hopelessness.

If ever anything seemed hopeless, it was
on the day of Jesus' crucifixion. The hopes
and dreams of those who thought that He
was the promised Messiah were shattered
when He died on the cross. But then God
intervened and miraculously turned ap-
parent defeat into victory. The sorrowful
Good Friday was transformed into the
triumphant resurrection of the Easter
Sunday – when Christ rose victoriously from
the grave.

Whatever circumstances you might
find yourself in, however dismal, always
remember that God is with you and that He
is in control of your circumstances.

*Redeemer and Friend, thank You that I can be
sure that God loves me and is always with me.
Amen.*

Your Will Be Done

"Yet not My will, but Yours be done."
Luke 22:42

Many things come our way in life – unexpected disappointments and trials – and often we cannot see any reason for them. But whether they are major or minor problems, we need to handle them all.

The Lord's love for us is endlessly tender and encouraging. He wants us to trust where we cannot see, and it will not be a reckless leap in the dark, as sincere trust and faith says, "I know for certain that God's will is best for me." This kind of faith leaves the choice up to God, with the words His Son taught us, "Your will be done!"

Eternal God and Father, thank You for sending Your Son to come and teach me what it means to let Your will be done in my life. Let Your Spirit assist me in this. Amen.

Through Him Who Strengthens Me

Blessed is the man who trusts in the Lord,
whose confidence is in Him.
Jeremiah 17:7

Everybody is searching for peace. No one can avoid the strain of life or the severe stress it brings with it. Jesus radiated love, serenity and peace; no matter how turbulent or chaotic the circumstances were around Him.

This was the result of His intimate relationship with His Father. Jesus regularly withdrew in solitude to pray and pour out His heart to His Father. Then He was able to return to a stormy life with the peace of heaven in His heart.

Whatever life may have in store for you, you will be victorious in His strength because, "I can do everything through Him who gives me strength" (Phil. 4:13).

You are my Keeper, O Lord. I place myself
under Your control and in Your care.
That is why I am assured of Your peace.
Amen.

I Know for Certain

He will never leave you nor forsake you.
Deuteronomy 31:6

It is important to have someone you can rely on and turn to in times of trouble. Yet sometimes even the closest friends can disappoint you.

Our Lord and Master will never let us down, however. If you need comfort, the Lord will comfort you. If you need guidance, the Lord will guide you. If you need inspiration for a difficult task, the Lord will inspire you.

If the road ahead of you seems to be strewn with problems, concerns and troubles, then ask the Lord to help you and you will discover that He is as faithful as His Word promises.

God my Father, thank You that I have the assurance
that You will never leave me nor forsake me.
Forgive me for the times when I've
failed and disappointed You.
Amen.

Christ's Peace – My Inheritance

"Peace I leave with you; My peace I give to you.
Not as the world gives do I give to you. Let not
your hearts be troubled, neither let it be afraid."
John 14:27 NKJV

This world's peace is a poor reflection of the peace that God gives to His children. The peace of God is the most wonderful peace imaginable. It affects every area of our lives. It is constant and does not change according to our moods.

But this peace requires a steadfast faith in Jesus Christ, who is the source of this peace. Such peace banishes worry, because that is the weapon the devil uses to undermine our peace. Jesus prohibits fear, because fear is the enemy of all peace.

*I praise and thank You for the peace that
conquers the fear and anxiety in my life.
Amen*

God's Peace Is Unfailing

Who is God besides the Lord?
And who is the Rock except our God?
2 Samuel 22:32

Often when people are experiencing problems, or if they need advice, they turn to a friend for help. But human effort always falls short.

If you find yourself in a difficult situation, don't underestimate the power and love of God.

Complete healing flows from an absolute and unconditional trust in, and surrender to, the living Christ. It doesn't matter what your problem is, the only lasting solution is to be found in the unfathomable love which God, through Jesus, bestowed on humanity.

Never be too proud or too afraid to turn to Jesus. Lay all your problems at His feet. He gave His life for you and will grant you the healing balm of His peace.

I want to hold on to You, Lord, when the storm
winds blow and I feel insecure. Grant me Your peace.
Amen.

The Center of Christ's Peace

*"Peace I leave with you; My peace I give you.
I do not give to you as the world gives. Do not
let your hearts be troubled and do not be afraid."*
John 14:27

Few people can honestly say that they do not long for peace of mind and inner tranquility. The troubles and pressures of life can drive many to seek comfort in different things; be it tranquilizers, drugs, professional help or even alcohol. Others simply give in to despair and just go through the motions of life.

The only proven way to handle the problems and tensions of life is by having a faith that is steadfastly grounded in the living Christ. Hold on to Him in all circumstances, talk to Him and, regardless of how desperate your situation might be, trust that He is always with you. His peace will then fill your heart, helping you overcome all your fears.

*Prince of Peace, please help me to turn to You
first in everything that happens to me today.
Amen.*

Peace in the Storm

*You will keep in perfect peace him whose
mind is steadfast, because he trusts in You.*
Isaiah 26:3

If you allow your thoughts to dwell on the things that are happening in the world today, you run the risk of being caught up in a whirlpool of hatred, bitterness and fear.

Yet, when your faith threatens to falter, God gives you the power to believe that all things will work out for the good of those who love Him. Peace is the direct result of trust. When your faith in God is sure, you receive an inner calm that brings balance to your life. Put God first in all things and you will know His peace and joy, even in the most trying circumstances.

*Almighty God, thank You that with You at the
center of my life I fear no storms, not even
problems as threatening as hurricanes.
Amen.*

The Blessing
of a Peacemaker

"Blessed are the peacemakers,
for they will be called sons of God."
Matthew 5:9

Peacemakers create healthy relationships. They are people in whose presence bitterness, hatred and unforgiveness simply cannot survive. They are children of God and aim to be at peace with all people.

To live in peace with friends is easy, but what about your enemies? Therefore it is peace at a risk: it includes peace with your enemies and persecutors.

Peacemakers are willing to venture something so that they can perform a deed of peace for the sake of Christ. To be a peacemaker is not a pious ideal or an unreachable dream; in Christ, it is an achievable goal through the help of the Holy Spirit.

Holy Spirit of God, enable me, for the sake of Jesus, my Lord, to be a peacemaker in this world.
Amen.

The Gift of Peace

"Peace I leave with you;
My peace I give to you."
John 14:27 NKJV

Jesus promises peace to His followers. Often God's blessings and peace are all that we desire here on earth to help us in our everyday lives.

The Lord does not want us to worry or lose hope because of things that are happening around us. That is why He promises to "bless His people with peace" (see Ps. 29:11).

The Lord does not force His gifts upon us, but He is always ready to grant them when we are ready to receive them. If we ask for peace in prayer, then the Lord will bless us with His peace in our innermost being so that we may experience His peace here on earth.

Savior and Prince of Peace, thank You that I know for certain that You have not only redeemed me, but that You have also granted me Your heavenly peace. Amen.

I will not fail you or abandon you. Be

strong the right o

strong and *courageous*, for you

Then you will be successful i

are the one who will lead these people to

you do. Study this Book o

possess all the land I swore to their ancestor:

continually. Meditate on it d

I would give them. Be *strong* and very

so you will be sure to obe

courageous. Be careful to obey all the

written in it. Only then will

instructions Moses gave you

and succeed in all you d

Do not deviate from them, turning either to

command be *strong* and *cour*

the right or to the left

Do not be afraid or

Then you will be successful in everything

For the Lord your Go

you do. Study this Book of Instruction

wherever you go. Josh. 1:5

continually. Meditate on it day and nigh

fail you or abandon you. Be *st*

so you will be sure to obey everything

courageous, for you are

written in it. Only then will you prospe

will lead these people to possess

and succeed in all you do. This is M

Protection

I will not fail you or abandon you. Be strong and courageous, for you are the one who will lead these people to possess all the land I swore to their ancestors I would give them. Be strong and very courageous. Be careful to obey all the instructions Moses gave you. Do not deviate from them, turning either to the right or to the left. Then you will be successful in everything you do. Study this Book of Instruction continually. Meditate on it day and night so you will be sure to obey everything written in it. Only then will you prosper and succeed in all you do. This is My command—be strong and courageous! Do not be afraid or discouraged. For the Lord your God is with you wherever you go. Josh. 1:5-9.

Protection

The Lord will keep you from all
harm – He will watch over your life.
Psalm 121:7

We can never drift out of the reach of God's love and omnipotence. He will never forsake us. His eyes continuously move over all the earth in order to help those who trust in Him. He shelters them in times of danger, helps them handle temptations and problems and comforts them in sorrow.

What a blessed privilege it is to have such a God as our protector. If we live within His will, wherever we find ourselves, we can rest assured that He keeps a loving watch over us and that He will hear when we call on Him.

It is a privilege to know that, wherever you may go, He constantly watches over you. If we walk in His path and do His will every moment of the day, we will have the assurance in our hearts that our Master and Savior is always near us to protect us and provide for us.

Promises of Protection

The Lord is my shepherd,
I shall not be in want.
He makes me lie down in green pastures,
He leads me beside quiet waters,
He restores my soul. He guides me in
paths of righteousness for His name's sake.
Even though I walk through the
valley of the shadow of death,
I will fear no evil, for You are with me;
Your rod and Your staff, they comfort me.
You prepare a table before me in the
presence of my enemies. You anoint my
head with oil; my cup overflows.
Surely goodness and love will
follow me all the days of my life, and I
will dwell in the house of the Lord forever.
Psalm 23

Let all those that put their trust in Thee
rejoice: let them ever shout for joy,
because Thou defendest them: let them
also that love Thy name be joyful in Thee.
Psalm 5:11 KJV

The angel of the Lord encamps all around
those who fear Him, and delivers them.
Oh, taste and see that the Lord is good;
blessed is the man who trusts in Him!
Psalm 34:7-8 NKJV

My God shall supply all your need according
to His riches in glory by Christ Jesus.
Philippians 4:19 NKJV

O Lord, You will keep us safe and
protect us from such people forever.
Psalm 12:7

"Because he holds fast to Me in love,
I will deliver him; I will protect him,
for he knows My name. When he calls to Me,
I will answer him; I will be with him in trou-
ble; I will rescue him and honor him."
Psalm 91:14-15 ESV

God is able to make all grace
abound to you, so that having all
sufficiency in all things at all times,
you may abound in every good work.
2 Corinthians 9:8 ESV

The Lord gives strength to His people;
the Lord blesses His people with peace.
Psalm 29:11

The Lord is my portion and my cup;
You hold my lot.
Psalm 16:5 ESV

Oh, fear the Lord, you His saints!
There is no want to those who fear Him.
The young lions lack and suffer hunger,
but those who seek the Lord shall
not lack any good thing.
Psalm 34:9-10 NKJV

"Fear thou not; for I am with thee: be not
dismayed; for I am thy God: I will strengthen
thee; yea, I will help thee; yea, I will uphold
thee with the right hand of My righteousness."
Isaiah 41:10 KJV

The name of the Lord is a strong tower;
the righteous run to it and are safe.
Proverbs 18:10

You are a hiding place for me;
You preserve me from trouble;
You surround me with shouts of deliverance.
Psalm 32:7 ESV

Surely He will save you from the fowler's
snare and from the deadly pestilence.
He will cover you with His feathers,
and under His wings you will find refuge;
His faithfulness will be your
shield and rampart.
Psalm 91:3-4

I will not fail you or abandon you. Be

strong the right or

strong and **courageous**, for you

Then you will be successful in

are the one who will lead these people to

you do. Study this Book of

possess all the land I swore to their ancestors

continually. Meditate on it da

I would give them. Be *strong* and very

so you will be sure to obey

courageous. Be careful to obey all the

written in it. Only then will

instructions Moses gave you

and succeed in all you do

Do not deviate from them, turning either to

command be *strong* and **cour**

the right or to the left.

Do not be afraid or d

Then you will be successful in everything

For the Lord your God

you do. Study this Book of Instruction

wherever you go. Josh. 1:5

continually. Meditate on it day and night

fail you or abandon you. Be *st*

so you will be sure to obey everything

courageous, for you are t

written in it. Only then will you prosper

will lead these people to possess

and succeed in all you do. This is My

Praise *and* Thanksgiving

Praise God!

*My heart is steadfast, O God; I will sing
and make music with all my soul.*
Psalm 108:1-2

We pray to thank God for what He has done for us, to lay our needs before Him, and to confess our sins to Him, but we often neglect to praise Him in our prayers.

Never underestimate the power of praise in your life. If someone impresses you, you praise him or her, so why shouldn't you shower God with your praise? He is indeed worthy of our love and thanksgiving.

If you focus on praising and glorifying God, you will create a very special relationship with the living Christ. Your prayer life will be transformed and your love for Him intensified. Through your praise you will become a stronger witness for Him.

*Great and wonderful God, we want to exalt
Your name and glorify You for all the wonders
of Your love and grace that You give to us.
Amen.*

The Blessing of a Grateful Heart

"He who sacrifices thank offerings honors Me."
Psalm 50:23

Sometimes a complaint is valid, but the danger of complaining is that it can become a habit. Eventually you forget that there are more things to be grateful for than to complain about. If you are complaining more often than you are expressing gratitude, then you are living an inferior quality of life.

Never let a day go by without consciously expressing your gratitude. Open your eyes to that which is beautiful around you and praise God for what you see and experience. When you start thanking God for His gifts of grace, He is already planning the next blessing for you.

Praise the Lord, O my soul, all my inmost being praise His holy name.
Amen.

The Blessing of Gratitude

Give thanks to the Lord, call on His name; make known among the nations what He has done.
1 Chronicles 16:8

In the hustle and bustle of everyday life it is easy to forget about ordinary courtesy. The habit of saying "Thank you" enriches every aspect of our lives. Always be ready to express thanks. You will soon discover how much joy you can bring to others. Apart from the fact that you enrich and bless the lives of others, your own life will be enriched. Never underestimate the power of gratitude.

All that we have, our heavenly Father has given to us. How much more will our lives be enriched if we learn to express gratitude toward Him?

Grant me a grateful heart, O God, for all the wondrous things that You have done for us, but above all, for the birth of Jesus, our Savior. Amen.

Rejoice in the Lord!

*Then the people of Israel – the priests,
the Levites and the rest of the exiles – celebrated
the dedication of the house of God with joy.*
Ezra 6:16

Many Christians see Christianity as somber and attend church simply out of a false sense of duty. Such an attitude tragically deprives them of the greatest of all joys: joy in the Lord.

God offers you fullness of life. Turn to Him and you will become more aware of His life-giving Spirit. As you open yourself up to the Holy Spirit, you will find that your worship, Bible study and prayer life gain new meaning. If you place your trust in the living Christ, you will discover that God is no longer a remote being, but an integral part of your life.

Worship ought to be a joyful experience. Open yourself to the Holy Spirit and He will raise you from despondency to ecstasy in Christ.

*O Holy Spirit, come into my life
and fill me with the joy of the Lord.
Amen.*

Think and Thank!

I thank my God every time I remember you.
Philippians 1:3

When the path of life becomes steep, and dark clouds threaten to block out all inspiration, pause a while and consider how God has brought you along thus far. Remember all His abundant blessings. At times disaster loomed and you might have felt that everything was lost, but God helped you rise from the ashes of failure.

The key that unlocks the door to a creative life is gratitude. With everything in life, look for something to be grateful for. When you assimilate this truth into your heart, you will approach the future with God-given confidence and the assurance that, in the name of Christ and in His strength, you can triumph over every situation.

Beloved Lord, I recall the blessings of the past
and the joys of the present. Thank You for
showers of blessings that You pour upon me.
Amen.

Gratitude Glorifies God

I will praise You, O Lord, with all my heart; I will tell of all Your wonders.
Psalm 9:1

Even though religion is a serious matter, some of God's most dedicated servants have been lively, happy people. A faith that is void of humor can hardly express the spirit and attitude of Jesus Christ.

One of the most beautiful things we read about Jesus is that ordinary people enjoyed listening to Him and children were at ease in His presence. This would not have been true had He been constantly gloomy. He emanated a deep peace and happiness – joy and quiet humor enabled Him to love and appreciate people.

Your sense of humor, enriched by your gratitude and love, is a gift from God.

I am so grateful for the way in which Jesus revealed You to us, Father. Thank You for being approachable and for Your great love.
Amen.

Be Thankful in Everything

Better a little with the fear of the Lord
than great wealth with turmoil.
Proverbs 15:16

The average Christian is so busy looking for a spectacular revelation of the miracle-working God that he is not able to see God at work in the common, everyday things.

When you have learned to appreciate the small blessings from God, you will see how God is at work in your life. The wonder of friendship, the kindness of strangers, and an understanding heart are all expressions of the greatness and the blessings of God.

Make a decision today to never again take anything for granted. Thank God for His blessings and you will unlock the treasure room of God and fill your life with new beauty and riches.

I praise and thank You, gracious Lord, for the small things that make each day so delightful. Help me never again to take daily blessings for granted. Amen.

Serve God with Gladness!

Worship the Lord with gladness;
come before Him with joyful songs.
Psalm 100:2

I praise and thank You, Father, because You created me and then made me a new creation in Christ. Thank You for the beauty of Creation through which You speak to me and where I can draw close to You in worship.

With gratitude I praise You for Your Word, through which the Holy Spirit reveals Your divine will for my life.

I praise and thank You for abundant blessings – for my family, my friends and all the things that make my life worthwhile. Give me a grateful heart always Lord, so that my life may be a song of thanksgiving to Your glory.

I want to sing to the glory of the Lord as long
as I live. You have done great things
and You are worthy of all praise.
Amen.

The Secret of a Festive Life

Always giving thanks to God the Father for everything, in the name of our Lord Jesus Christ.
Ephesians 5:20

If Jesus Christ abides in you through faith, you develop a keener appreciation of the beauty and depth hidden in the lives of others, as well as in the world around you. The greater your gratitude, the more life will reveal its hidden treasures to you.

It is important to be thankful. All through Scripture we hear the resounding echo of the praise of those who loved God and were grateful for His blessings. We appreciate the blessings, but we love God because He is our Father. Our hearts overflow with gratitude for all He does for us.

Thank You, Lord Jesus, for all Your love
and gifts that You have granted me.
Amen.

All the Earth Bows Down to You

How awesome are Your deeds! So great is Your power that Your enemies cringe before You. All the earth bows down to You.
Psalm 66:3-4

The believer need not have any doubt that God answers prayer! And when He does, we should sing His praises and thank Him for His faithfulness.

Today's psalm was written after Israel had won a war under difficult circumstances. The Israelites wanted to testify to each other, to the world, and to God Himself, how great and mighty He is – so that everyone would bow before Him.

To be on God's side is the greatest privilege on earth. Let us thank God with our whole heart because we know He hears our prayers and will always cause us to triumph over our enemies!

We bow in thankfulness before You God.
Thank You for everything You have done for us!
Amen.

Spiritual Blessings

Praise be to the God and
Father of our Lord Jesus Christ,
who has blessed us in the heavenly realms
with every spiritual blessing in Christ.
For He chose us in Him before the creation of
the world to be holy and blameless in His sight.
Ephesians 1:3-4

We should regularly praise and thank God for all the spiritual blessings that He gives to us, such as our salvation and our inheritance in heaven.

Praise Him also for the spiritual blessings that you cannot see, such as joy, inner happiness and hope in your heart. Give praise and worship to our merciful God from whom all our spiritual blessings come.

When the pressures and troubles of life are weighing down on you, praise God for the abundance of His blessings that He gives you daily.

Merciful and loving Lord, I praise Your holy name for all the spiritual blessings in my life. Amen.

My Lips Will Shout for Joy

I will praise You with the harp for Your
faithfulness, O my God; I will sing praise to
You with the lyre, O Holy One of Israel.
My lips will shout for joy when
I sing praise to You.
Psalm 71:22-23

The writer of these Scripture verses describes himself as old, saying that his strength has failed. But after he had examined his life thoughtfully and prayerfully, this "old" person was bubbling over with joy. He sings the praises of God and brings to remembrance everything that God has done for him.

Far too often we find ourselves praying hesitant prayers to God and our songs of praise are rather half-hearted. Offer up enthusiastic praise to God and feel the joy of the Lord that will stir inside you.

*Lord, my God and Father, I will praise
You with thanksgiving and singing
and tell others of Your wonderful deeds.
Amen.*

The Lamb Is Worthy to Receive Our Praise

Then I looked and heard the voice of many
angels. In a loud voice they sang:
"Worthy is the Lamb!"
Revelation 5:11-12

The Bible encourages Christians to offer prayers of praise and thanksgiving, which reveal their commitment to God.

Yes, our private devotions are very important, but there is an element missing unless we join together with other believers to praise God. We are fulfilling our calling as worshipers when we, God's children, are caught up in worshiping Him.

It is, after all, from worshipers of every place and age that Christ will receive the worship He so richly deserves. May God help us continuously to be found in the company of praying people.

Lord Jesus, blessing and honor, glory and power,
belong to You. I pray for the company of other
believers so that we can praise Your name together.
Amen.

Purpose *and* Potential

Purpose and Potential

He who has prepared us for this very thing is
God, who has given us the Spirit as a guarantee.
2 Corinthians 5:5 ESV

For many people life is nothing but a monotonous routine. Day in and day out they go through the motions and constantly wonder if life has any meaning. Others are ambitious and want to reach the top in their profession, but often sacrifice integrity in order to obtain riches and prestige.

But there comes a time when every person starts seeking the real meaning of life. The only satisfying answer is a spiritual one. People who have a sincere and vibrant relationship with the living Christ have found the answer to this question. They live a purposeful life through the power of Christ.

The glorious truth is that people were created to glorify, worship and serve God. When God is at the center of a life, He pours out His blessing and life begins to reveal its deep secrets. When your purpose in life is to serve God and your fellow man, you discover the deeper meaning of life.

Lasting Purpose and True Potential

Now to each one the manifestation of the Spirit is given for the common good. To one there is given through the Spirit the message of wisdom, to another the message of knowledge by means of the same Spirit, to another faith by the same Spirit, to another gifts of healing by that one Spirit, to another miraculous powers, to another prophecy, to another distinguishing between spirits, to another speaking in different kinds of tongues, and to still another the interpretation of tongues. All these are the work of one and the same Spirit, and He gives them to each one, just as He determines.
1 Corinthians 12:7-11

I can do all things through
Him who strengthens me.
Philippians 4:13 ESV

I am sure of this, that He who began
a good work in you will bring it to
completion at the day of Jesus Christ.
Philippians 1:6 ESV

Therefore, my beloved, as you have
always obeyed, not as in my presence only,
but now much more in my absence,
work out your own salvation with fear and
trembling; for it is God who works in you
both to will and to do for His good pleasure.
Philippians 2:12-13 NKJV

That He might make known the
riches of His glory on the vessels of mercy,
which He had afore prepared unto glory,
even us, whom He hath called, not of
the Jews only, but also of the Gentiles?
Romans 9:23-24 KJV

We know that all things work together
for good to those who love God, to those
who are the called according to His purpose.
Romans 8:28 NKJV

Trust in the Lord with all thine heart;
and lean not unto thine own understanding.
In all thy ways acknowledge Him,
and He shall direct thy paths.
Proverbs 3:5-6 KJV

Teach me to do Your will, for You are my
God; Your Spirit is good. Lead me in
the land of uprightness.
Psalm 143:10 NKJV

You are my lamp, O Lord; the Lord
turns my darkness into light.
With Your help I can advance against
a troop; with my God I can scale a wall.
2 Samuel 22:29-30

He made known to us the mystery of His
will according to His good pleasure, which He
purposed in Christ, to be put into effect when
the times will have reached their fulfillment –
to bring all things in heaven and on earth
together under one head, even Christ.
Ephesians 1:9-10

"For this purpose I have raised you up,
to show you My power, so that My name
may be proclaimed in all the earth."
Exodus 9:16 ESV

The counsel of the Lord stands forever,
the plans of His heart to all generations.
Psalm 33:11 NKJV

I will cry unto God most high;
unto God that performeth all things for me.
Psalm 57:2 KJV

For surely, O Lord, You bless the righteous;
You surround them with Your
favor as with a shield.
Psalm 5:12

I will not fail you or abandon you. B

strong

the right o

strong and *courageous*, for yo

Then you will be successful i

are the one who will lead these people t

you do. Study this Book o

possess all the land I swore to their ancestor

continually. Meditate on it d

I would give them. Be *strong* and ver

so you will be sure to obe

courageous. Be careful to obey all th

written in it. Only then will

instructions Moses gave you

and succeed in all you d

Do not deviate from them, turning either t

command be *strong* and *cour*

the right or to the left

Do not be afraid or

Then you will be successful in everything

For the Lord your Go

you do. Study this Book of Instructio

wherever you go. Josh. 1:5

continually. Meditate on it day and nigh

fail you or abandon you. Be *sl*

so you will be sure to obey everything

courageous, for you are

written in it. Only then will you prospe

will lead these people to possess

and succeed in all you do. This is M

Praying Power

Prayer: The Challenge

Being in anguish, He prayed more earnestly.
Luke 22:44

There are enriching moments in prayer when you experience glorious intimacy with God and are filled with inexpressible joy. But true prayer often has a seriousness that touches on the deeper issues of life.

When you pray that God will help you grow spiritually, or show you the right way to live, or use you in His service, you will experience the full impact of the challenge of prayer.

Such prayers are essentially between you and God, but you will soon discover that they touch other people as well. As God lays people on your heart, you begin to understand the responsibility of prayer. Sharing in this privilege strengthens you to live in love towards God and your fellow man.

Lord, I pray that my heart would be overwhelmed
by the love of God so that I can truly
love and pray for those around me.
Amen.

Pray for Discernment

Your righteousness is everlasting and Your law is true. Trouble and distress have come upon me, but Your commands are my delight.

Psalm 119:142-143

The trials and tribulations of life often force us to turn to someone or something for help. The psalmist, however, knew it was best to turn to God for wisdom and discernment.

He asked of God, "Give me understanding that I may live." He knew that God's plan for his life would preserve him from wrongful actions and would destroy the path of the foolish. Therefore he chose to delight himself in God and to uphold His statutes. God promises to grant us wisdom if we ask Him for it (James 1:5).

Pray to God for discernment and wisdom in your struggle and ask Him to teach you what you need to know so you can apply His wisdom to your situation.

Heavenly Father, I am Your redeemed servant and I ask for wisdom and discernment. Amen.

Take Time to Pray

None of us lives to himself alone.
Romans 14:7

People always find the time to do the things they want to do, but are quick to find excuses for not doing the things they don't want to do. This happens in our spiritual lives too.

If you are making excuses as to why you can't pray or spend time with God, ask yourself why you are making these excuses. Why is your prayer life without power? Why has your faith become a burden instead of an inspiration of hope and faith?

This happens when you no longer reach out to God in prayer, or if you only ever express your personal desires. True prayer broadens your spiritual and intellectual horizons, and makes your relationship with the Savior more profound.

O Lord, please help me to develop a
meaningful and powerful prayer life
under the guidance of the Holy Spirit.
Amen.

Pray – Regardless ...

When my life was ebbing away,
I remembered You, Lord, and my prayer
rose to You, to Your holy temple.
Jonah 2:7

Many people deny themselves the privilege of the peace of God, simply because they feel too undeserving to talk to God.

Yet Jesus promised that He will not cast out anybody who comes to Him. He also emphasized that He did not come to call the righteous, but sinners, to salvation. Throughout the Scriptures you can read of His unfathomable mercy and endless love that reach out to all people: the good and the bad, the worthy and the unworthy.

However unworthy you may feel at this moment, reach out to Him in prayer and He will take you by the hand – and nobody will snatch you from Him.

Father, I want to live my life glorifying You. Help me not to lose sight of You when times are difficult. Guide me towards obedience through Your Spirit. Amen.

Make Prayer Your Motivational Power

"When you pray, do not keep on
babbling like pagans, for they think they
will be heard because of their many words."
Matthew 6:7

There are many people who do not give serious thought to their prayers to God. They have a fixed pattern that used to be meaningful but through repetition has lost its meaning.

When you spend time in the presence of the living God, and you are sharing your wishes with Him, you must be seriously mindful of the guidance of the Holy Spirit. Ask Him while you pray if there is anything that you can do to make your prayer life more fertile. Believe in your prayers and then leave everything in God's hands and see how He works in your life.

*Father, through Christ I wish to glorify You
as my Father. Grant that I, through the
guidance of Your Holy Spirit, may be
obedient in my quiet times with You.
Amen.*

Be Patient in Prayer

I will stand at my watch and station
myself on the ramparts; I will look to
see what He will say to me, and what
answer I am to give to this complaint.
Habakkuk 2:1

So often people complain that their prayers remain unheard. They become impatient with God and their faith weakens.

Yet it is an established and irrefutable fact that God hears and answers our prayers. However, we need to know His Word to understand that His answer comes in His perfect time, and in His perfect way, according to His perfect will. This is also done according to our needs – not our wishes and will, unless they are in accordance with God.

Truly effective prayer often requires us to watch and wait. He will reveal Himself to us and show us His way in His good time.

*Father, grant that in times of doubt I will turn to
You, that I will hold on to Your constancy and on
to the assurance that I have in Jesus Christ.
Amen.*

Wisdom Comes through Prayer

*If any of you lacks wisdom, he should ask God,
who gives generously to all without
finding fault; and it will be given to him.*
James 1:5

Prayer holds many advantages for those who make it part of their daily routine. To wait patiently in the presence of God creates an opportunity to experience the Holy Spirit. It can transform a time of senseless words into a source of strength and wisdom that restores balance to your life.

God talks to you through prayer. Whether you are plagued by doubt or confusion, or whether you are finding it difficult to make a decision, the person who prays will be enlightened and guided. Prayer confirms the existence of God in your heart and brings with it a new experience of life and wisdom.

*Jesus, Savior, Your burden is light and
Your yoke is easy. Help me to take up
my cross daily and follow You.
Amen.*

Miracles through Prayer

Praise be to the Lord, for He has heard my cry for mercy. The Lord is my strength and my shield; my heart trusts in Him, and I am helped.
Psalm 28:6-7

Despite the cynicism of our age, God can still perform miracles. Every time someone is healed in answer to prayer, God has performed a miracle. Every time we experience peace in our hearts after a time of tension and suffering, or when our grief finally becomes bearable – then a miracle has occurred.

Hand your problems over to God in prayer today and wait on Him in faith. If there is something you need to do, do it without delay. Do not let despair overwhelm you. In the right time and in the right way, God will answer your prayers and you will be astounded by the results.

My God and Father, I know that You are powerful and that You can do far more than I can pray for or think of because You are the Almighty.
Amen.

The Prayer of Jesus

After Jesus said this, He looked toward heaven
and prayed: "Father, the time has come.
Glorify Your Son, that Your Son
may glorify You."
John 17:1

In preparation for the suffering that Jesus
knew He would have to endure in the days
ahead, He prayed for God to be glorified in
His body at the Last Supper.

How could a terrible death on the cross
bring glory to God? Jesus explains in His
prayer that God is glorified through the
obedience of the Son. We seldom feel that
our suffering and defeat could be to God's
glory, yet we seldom look at things from a
godly perspective.

God's glory is reflected in our deeds of
love, obedience and loyalty. Follow Jesus'
example today by praying that God will be
glorified in your life and by your obedience.

*Loving Father, help me to contribute
to the glory of Your name by doing
everything in obedience to Your will.
Amen.*

Come, Let Us Pray

There on the beach we knelt to pray.
Acts 21:5

There are people who believe that prayer should be limited to the church or to the privacy of an inner room. They regard any form of public prayer with uneasiness and even disapproval.

Yet prayer is as much a form of communication as a conversation is. Except prayer is a conversation between our heavenly Father and us. There is nothing more natural than this.

While you should never be too shy to pray, it is also necessary to be discreet in terms of the time and place you choose to pray.

Trust in the guidance of the Holy Spirit and your prayers will always be a blessing to you as well as to others.

O Hearer of prayers, thank You that
I can draw near to Your sacred throne
at all times and under all circumstances,
and I know that You will always listen.
Amen.

The Path of Prayer

"When you pray, do not keep on
babbling like pagans, for they think they
will be heard because of their many words.
Do not be like them, for your Father
knows what you need before you ask Him."
Matthew 6:7-8

Repetitive prayers may be a good way to develop the spirit of prayer, but the Lord makes it abundantly clear that prayer becomes ineffective when it deteriorates into the mere recital of pretty phrases.

True prayer is more than words. It is an attitude of the spirit and mind that reaches out to God. Prayer is a two-way process. You tell God what you want from Him and He reveals to you what He expects from you. Prayer is not a series of empty words, but rather an increasingly intimate relationship with the heavenly Father and a sincere desire to do His will.

*God and Father, grant me the true spirit of prayer
so that my communion with You will become
more and more profound and meaningful.
Amen.*

The Gracious Gift of Prayer

Devote yourselves to prayer,
being watchful and thankful.
Colossians 4:2

What value do you place on prayer? Do you regard it as a wonderful gift of grace from God, or as an unbearable burden?

The privilege of prayer is a special gift from God to us. It is God's personal invitation to you to enter into His sanctuary, to talk to Him and listen when He has something to say to you.

Prayer is a discipline that requires preparation and practice. Make time to come quietly into the presence of God. Focus your attention on Jesus. Listen and speak to God and thank Him for the gracious gift of His love for you. That will enable you to live in an atmosphere of peace and trust.

Lord, thank You for the privilege of being able to bring every aspect of my life to You in prayer. Amen.

Prepare Yourself for Life through Prayer

Pray without ceasing.
1 Thessalonians 5:17

The future is unknown but you can prepare for it by developing a healthy prayer life. This will provide you with strength in moments of weakness, and comfort in times of sorrow.

Many people will tell you that praying is a natural instinct. This may be true, but an effective prayer life is the result of a disciplined and sensitive attitude before God.

Share your joy with God in prayer while the sun shines and there will be no anxiety when the storm comes. You will merely share in the quiet conviction that God is in full control and that you have prepared adequately for every situation in life through prayer. God will do the rest!

How wonderful, heavenly Father, to praise and glorify You. I want to sing the praises of Your great love and faithfulness for all nations to hear. Amen.

Righteousness

Righteousness

"Blessed are those who hunger and thirst
for righteousness, for they shall be satisfied."
Matthew 5:6 ESV

The Bible tells us clearly that we are all sinners and that we all fall short of the glory of God. But if you ask God to forgive your sins, it is futile to constantly remind yourself of them. If God has forgiven you, you must forgive yourself.

When God forgave your sins, He made you new, "Therefore, if anyone is in Christ, he is a new creation; the old has gone, the new has come. All this is from God" (2 Cor. 5:17-18).

God made you new and the righteousness that He gave you should have a positive influence on your life. Allow God's goodness to take root and to grow in you.

When the Master saves you and gives you His Spirit, He also gives you a dynamic goodness that is a rich blessing to you and to all those around you.

Assured Righteousness

He believed the Lord, and He
accounted it to him for righteousness.
Genesis 15:6 NKJV

The work of righteousness shall be
peace; and the effect of righteousness
quietness and assurance for ever.
Isaiah 32:17 KJV

"Seek first the kingdom of God
and His righteousness, and all
these things shall be added to you."
Matthew 6:33 NKJV

This righteousness from God comes through
faith in Jesus Christ to all who believe.
There is no difference, for all have sinned
and fall short of the glory of God, and are
justified freely by His grace through the
redemption that came by Christ Jesus.
Romans 3:22-24

For Christ also hath once suffered for sins,
the just for the unjust, that He might bring
us to God, being put to death in the flesh,
but quickened by the Spirit.
1 Peter 3:18

For surely, O Lord, You bless the righteous;
You surround them with Your
favor as with a shield.
Psalm 5:12

Many are the afflictions of the righteous,
but the Lord delivers him out of them all.
Psalm 34:19 NKJV

The path of the righteous is
like the light of dawn, which shines
brighter and brighter until full day.
Proverbs 4:18 ESV

It shall be our righteousness, if we observe
to do all these commandments before the
Lord our God, as He hath commanded us.
Deuteronomy 6:25 KJV

The righteous will shine forth as the
sun in the kingdom of their Father.
He who has ears to hear, let him hear!
Matthew 13:43 NKJV

Henceforth there is laid for me the
crown of righteousness, which the Lord,
the righteous judge, will award to me on
that Day, and not only to me but also
to all who have loved His appearing.
2 Timothy 4:8 ESV

For our sake He made Him to be sin
who knew no sin, so that in Him we might
become the righteousness of God.
2 Corinthians 5:21 ESV

What is more, I consider everything a
loss compared to the surpassing greatness
of knowing Christ Jesus my Lord,
for whose sake I have lost all things.
I consider them rubbish,
that I may gain Christ and be found in Him,
not having a righteousness of my own that
comes from the law, but that which is
through faith in Christ – the righteousness
that comes from God and is by faith.
Philippians 3:8-9

Now the fruit of righteousness is sown
in peace by those who make peace.
James 3:18 NKJV

For the Lord knows the way of the righteous,
but the way of the wicked will perish.
Psalm 1:6 ESV

For the Lord God is a sun and shield;
the Lord bestows favor and honor;
no good thing does He withhold
from those whose walk is blameless.
Psalm 84:11

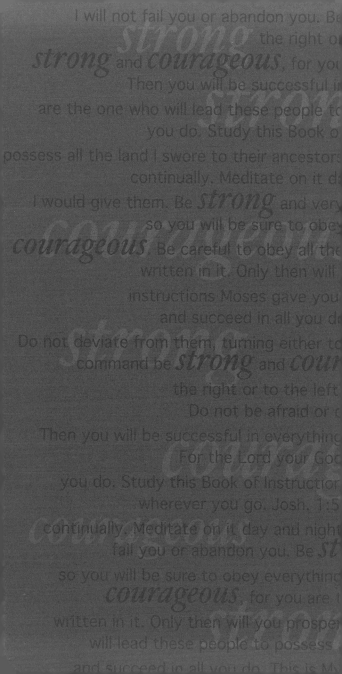

True Love

God's Redeeming Love

To them God has chosen to make known among
the Gentiles the glorious riches of this mystery,
which is Christ in you, the hope of glory.
Colossians 1:27

The wonder and glory of the Christian gospel
is that God loved us while we were still
sinners. Without such a love we would indeed have still been lost.

As you become deeply aware of your
imperfections and sin, you are also aware that
there is a divine and all-powerful Deity who is
calling you to a better and nobler life. Because
of our sinfulness it is impossible to live life as
God intended for us without His help.

So accept God's offer to recreate and
transform your life. Allow the Holy Spirit to
fill you with the strength you need to walk
according to God's ways.

*Lord, I am sincerely grateful that You bore my
punishment for sin and opened the way for me to
come to the Father and live according to His ways.
Amen.*

True Love

Love must be sincere.
Romans 12:9

The word love is probably the most used and least understood word in any language.

Jesus Christ came to demonstrate the meaning of true love when He willingly gave His life for all humanity. He took our punishment upon Himself to redeem us from our sinfulness. As He said, "Greater love has no one than this, that he lay down his life for his friends" (John 15:13).

True love involves making sacrifices for the sake of another. It is tolerant, patient and understanding, even in the most trying circumstances. It involves forgiveness and giving of yourself for the benefit of others. It means to love others as Jesus loves you.

Loving Lord Jesus, help me to spread
Your love in the world around me.
Amen.

Spirit of Love

Hope does not disappoint us, because God
has poured out His love into our hearts
by the Holy Spirit, whom He has given us.
Romans 5:5

Jesus promised His Holy Spirit to everyone
who accepts Him as Lord and Savior and He
has kept this promise.

Remember that Christ can change
your life. As you open your heart to Him,
a new unsurpassed strength will fill your
soul and enable you to do those things that
are pleasing to God. This change and new
strength are the work of the Spirit and will
assure you of Christ's presence in your life.

If you have the Spirit of Christ you will
know the reality of His holy presence. Love
for Him will radiate from your heart and life.

*I praise You, Lord, because I can experience
the power of Your living presence through
the work of the Holy Spirit and
so I can love You with a pure heart.
Amen.*

God's Great Gift

May the grace of the Lord Jesus Christ,
and the love of God, and the fellowship
of the Holy Spirit be with you all.
2 Corinthians 13:14

When we reflect on the sacrifice God made on Golgotha, through Jesus Christ, for our redemption and salvation, the eternal hope that He gave us through His triumphant resurrection from the dead and the power He extends to us through the Holy Spirit, we are overwhelmed with wonder.

There is no way we could ever repay the Lord for His immeasurable love. But we could, and should, open our lives to Him so that we can pass on His love to others. Christ commanded us to love one another as we love ourselves, and as He loves us.

*Lord, I want to glorify You as my Father always.
Guide me, through Your Holy Spirit, so that I
will be obedient to You in everything I do.
Amen.*

God's Love Has No Price

Peter answered: "May your money perish
with you, because you thought you
could buy the gift of God with money!"
Acts 8:20

Many people believe that money can buy them everything. While this may be true of material possessions, it cannot buy things like peace, joy and fullness of life. These qualities have no price tags. They are God's gifts of grace to us.

We enjoy everything that is good and worthwhile by the grace of God. We don't deserve these things, we cannot earn them and we are not worthy of them, but we receive them because of Christ's unfathomable love and grace towards us.

Never take the blessings that you receive from His hand for granted. Always remember that they are gifts of God's eternal goodness and a sign of His love towards you.

*I want to thank You for the undeserved gifts
that You bestow so graciously on my life –
for love and peace and hope.
Amen.*

Incredible but True

Now these three remain: faith, hope and love.
But the greatest of these is love.
1 Corinthians 13:13

In these troublesome times, when bitterness and prejudice abound, it is hard to remember that love triumphs. Thousands of years ago, Christ was unjustly tried and mocked by the Roman soldiers and cruelly nailed to a wooden cross.

Our awe of Christ on the cross lies in the fact that in the midst of public scorn, derision and unbearable pain, He prayed for those who crucified Him. His love surpassed all the powers of hatred.

When crime and violence make a mockery of all that Jesus Christ lived for and taught, then remember Golgotha and focus on God's love. You will find peace and calm that will make you aware of the immortality and invincibility of love.

God, I ask that love will be the motivating
factor of my life, as it is for Yours.
Amen.

Surrounded by God's Love

*"For them I sanctify Myself,
that they too may be truly sanctified."*
John 17:19

There are probably times in your life when your Christian walk seems like a struggle and your faith grows weak. When this happens, shift your focus and look at your life from Christ's viewpoint. His involvement in your life of faith is more important than your own. He is the one who called you.

This divine calling does not depend on your shifting emotions. He will bind you to Him with cords of love. When you become despondent, remember that the loving Christ will never change. You still belong to Him, He loves you and He is still your Lord. Christ's love for you doesn't change according to your emotions; it is eternal and unfailing.

*I thank You, O Guide, that my changing
emotions need not dictate the course of my life.
Thank You that Your love for me is constant.
Amen.*

Sincere Love

Love must be sincere.
Romans 12:9

Although we may doubt the sincerity of people's love, we need never doubt the sincerity of God's love for us. Love compelled Him to come to this world in the person of Jesus Christ and suffer and die on our behalf.

It was love that gave Him the victory over death and made Him ascend to heaven where He intercedes for us. It was love that urged Him to forgive our sins and offer us the gift of His Holy Spirit.

This world will never know any love greater than that of Jesus Christ. He gave us the example of sincere love and urges us to love as He loved.

*God of love, please help me to never
lose sight of the greatness of Your love for me,
no matter what happens in my life.
Amen.*

Love without Boundaries

They crucified Him. Dividing up His clothes,
they cast lots to see what each would get.
Mark 15:24

Throughout the ages people have rejected, ignored, denied and betrayed Jesus. Yet despite this, in times of need they still call on Him and ask for His help.

The marvel of the Christian faith is that regardless of how you treat Christ, He still loves you. He lavishes His boundless love on you and meets your needs.

The crucifixion shows us that the love of Christ knows no boundaries. It is a love so sincere and pure that nothing can withstand it. Whether you deserve it or not – this is the love that God wants to give to you through Jesus Christ. How then can you withhold your love from Him?

Lord, I want to share in the glory of Your love.
Fill me with Your love so that I can
truly love You as You deserve.
Amen.

God Loves You

We know that in all things God works for the good of those who love Him, who have been called according to His purpose.

Romans 8:28

People often cannot understand why trials and setbacks happen to them. Yet one of the basic components of Christianity is steadfast faith in the love of God. This love has been proven beyond a doubt in the gift of His Son to a lost world. That is why in every situation of life, you can put your trust in the wisdom and goodness of a loving Father.

When you find yourself facing problems or setbacks, remember that your life is in God's mighty hands. Because of His great love for you, everything that happens to you has a purpose.

Jesus, in the darkest moments of my life, thank You that I can be assured of the goodness of Your love that lets nothing happen to me by chance. Amen.

Love Is Practical and Sincere

This is how God showed His love among us:
He sent His one and only Son into the
world that we might live through Him.
1 John 4:9

Jesus Christ was deeply practical. If you study His life you will note that, along with the profound spirituality of His ministry, He had a truly practical nature. When Jesus raised Jairus's daughter from the dead, He told her parents to give her something to eat.

True love and care requires more than mere words – it calls for action. It is to support someone in prayer, but also to do something practical to show your love; even if it is inconvenient.

By demonstrating your love for others in a practical way, you follow the example Jesus set for us. He is our example because His love exceeds all other love.

Holy Jesus, help me to love others with a
love that is practical and sincere.
Amen.

Love Is the Most Excellent Way

Now I will show you the most excellent way.
1 Corinthians 12:31

Jesus was the embodiment of God's perfect love. He calls us to walk the path of this love. No compromise can be tolerated. If we wish to follow the most excellent way, we must follow the way of His love.

A response to the challenge of Christian love calls for deep devotion. Even when you have given everything, you still want to give more. It is then that you open your life to the influence of the Holy Spirit. That which you cannot achieve by your own effort and strength, God will achieve through you.

His Holy Spirit residing in us makes the impossible possible. Choose the best – choose to love!

Lord, reveal Your love in my life so that
I may love my neighbor. Help me to
aspire to this commandment of Yours.
Amen.

The Song of Love

If I speak in the tongues of men and of angels,
but have not love, I am only a resounding
gong or a clanging cymbal.
1 Corinthians 13:1

This chapter unlocks all the noble qualities of love. Here, Paul speaks about the path of love. He begins by saying that one can possess any spiritual gift, but if it does not bear the stamp of love, it is useless.

If love is not part of miracles, of sacrifice, or of our spoken and intellectual gifts, then they are fruitless. The gift of intellectual excellence without love leads to intellectual snobbery. Knowledge lit by the fire of love is the only kind of knowledge that can save people. None of these are worth anything if they do not go hand-in-hand with true love.

Lord, my God, I thank You that all the love in my
life is but a mere stepping stone towards You.
Amen.

Love Forgets about Self

Love does not boast.
1 Corinthians 13:4

Boasting is a negative form of love, called self-love. True love is selfless. It would rather confess unworthiness than boast of its own achievements. Some people give their love as though they were bestowing an honor on the receiver. That is not love; that is conceit.

The one that truly loves cannot stop marveling at the fact that there is someone who loves him. Love is kept humble in the knowledge that it could never make a sufficiently worthy sacrifice for the one it loves.

This also applies to our spiritual lives. We dare not accept God's love as a matter of course as if we deserved it. Such pride robs us of the blessing and spiritual growth that God has in mind for us.

Lord, keep me humble in my love, so that it does not become the cause of pride and arrogance. Amen.

Best-loved Promises
from God's Word

_____

_____

_____

_____

_____

_____

_____

_____

_____

_____

_____

_____

_____

_____

_____

_____

_____

_____

Best-loved Promises
from God's Word

_____

_____

_____

_____

_____

_____

_____

_____

_____

_____

_____

_____

_____

_____

_____

_____

Notes

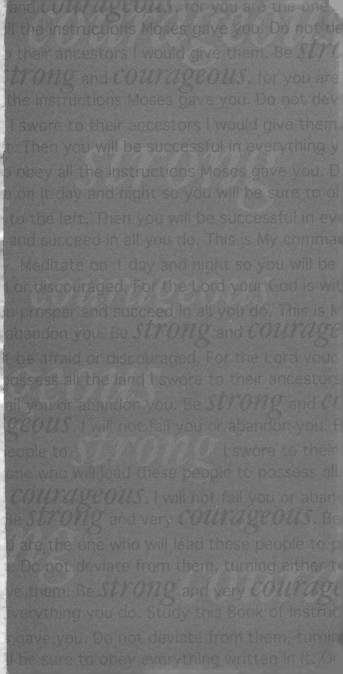

...I will not fail you or abandon you. Be strong and very courageous. Be careful to o... lead these people to possess all the land I sw... who will strong or abandon you and very courageous. Be careful to ob... strong lead these people to possess all the... from them, turning either to the right or to t... deviate and very courageous. Be car... Study this Book of Instruction continually. M... you everything written in it. Only then will you pr... to obey. Study this Book of Instruction cont... strong and courageous! Do not be ...mand be everything written in it. Only then w... wherever you go. Josh. 1:5-9. I will not fail yo... with you strong and courageous! f... for you are the one who will lead these peopl... ...geous, wherever you go. Josh. 1:5-9. I will ... would give them. Be strong and very co... ...cestors I, for you are the one who will lead th... strong and courageous, for you are ... you. Be would give them. Be strong and ... land I swore to their ancestors I would give th... ...ss all the strong and courageous, ... careful to obey all the instructions Moses gav... ...ous. Be and I swore to their ancestors I wo... right or to the left. Then you will be success... ...er to the careful to obey all the instructions ... continually. Meditate on it day and night so...